SOMEBODY
THAT WO

Best Wishes,
Christie Gibson

SOMEBODY SAID
THAT WORD

Edited by Chrissie Gittins
Preface by Sheila Hancock

LITTLEWOOD
1991

Published by Littlewood Arc
The Nanholme Centre, Shaw Wood Road,
Todmorden, Lancs. OL14 6DA

Copyright © 1991 Springhill Hospice, Rochdale

Design & print by The Arc & Throstle Press, Todmorden.
Typeset by Lasertext Limited, Stretford, Manchester.

ISBN 0946407 58 4

Acknowledgements for funding for the project and/or
publication are due to:
North West Arts,
Arts Council of Great Britain,
Hospice Arts,
The Paul Hamlyn Foundation and
The Granada Foundation.

Thanks are due to Marcus Ward for the cover
illustration — an interpretation of the "Resolution of
Pain".

Contents

	Preface	7
	Introduction	8
1	Brenda Kenyon	11
2	Tommy Dutton	14
3	Ted Worthington	15
4	Ann Howson	17
5	Bill Wheeler	18
6	Beatrice Marriott and Irene Hilton	23
7	Stanley Wyers	23
8	Betty Portman	25
9	Denis Norminton	27
10	Cora Margerison	27
11	Elaine Harling and Gladys Storey	29
12	Mary Redmond	31
13	Vivienne Travis	35
14	Margaret Macdonald	36
15	Marie Gibbon	38
16	Zeriah Moore	40
17	Marylyn and Kenneth Beaumont	45
18	Sidney Thomason	47
19	Margaret Geoghegan	47
20	Violet Davies	51
21	Dorothy Taylor	53
22	Lilian Owinor	54
23	Dr Gartside	55
24	Vanessa Tonks	58
25	George Kearton	59
26	Ivy Ashton	60
27	Ian Thompson	60
28	Ernest Prestwood	62
29	Kay Scott	62
30	Joan Cooper	66
31	Pam Harris	67
32	Mary Evans	68
	Useful Addresses	72

Preface

I am grateful to this book. I approached it with trepidation, thinking that work by people who are gravely ill and others who are caring for them, would be a depressing document. Not a bit of it. At a time when there is so much to appal us in the world, these uplifting tales are shining evidence that people are wonderful. Just that. Full of wonder. I marvel, in this 'Me, Me' society at the utter selflessness of the men and women portrayed here. No word of complaint for hard lives, want or pain, just gratitude and concern for others. With Chrissie Gittins' careful guidance they have produced a little treasure that gives you the same vivid characters and evocative social background as reading Dickens.

I spent a year in Oldham in the 50's and reading this brought back to me all the warmth and hardship that I witnessed then. It should be required reading for history students. And social science students. And students of life. And medical students. Especially them. The medical profession too often turns away from those they cannot cure and this book demonstrates yet again something I have seen so often in my work in hospices – that death can be made a good experience for everyone involved. It comforts me that someone like Vi, after what I, not she, judge to be an unfairly harsh life, can say of the hospice that "You never see a long face coming". I hope the contributors found as much pleasure in discovering their talent for story-telling as I have from reading their work.

Sheila Hancock

Introduction

The first patient I talked to was Jane. Had she ever thought of doing any writing? "Oh no." She had some cards to write, but didn't seem to be able to "get the go." Did she want me to help her? "Oh no." She'd do them later. We chatted on. She lived near a park where I'd fed ducks as a child. She's seen buildings go up in Rochdale and then get pulled down. When I said I'd better carry on she said, "Well, I hope you can find someone who can help you, love."

From the end of October 1990, I spent three days a week for six months at Springhill Hospice, Rochdale. It was part of a project set up by Hospice Arts, and funded by the Arts Council and North West Arts. Springhill is a purpose-built hospice which opened in October 1989. It can accommodate up to twenty in-patients, including one bed for a child, and offers a day-care service on Thursdays. Springhill operates a short stay policy. Patients who are well enough, and who have enough support, go home after a two to three week stay. Some patients return two, three, sometimes four times.

Jane put me right. I wasn't there to impose my views of what 'creative writing' might be, on patients who were often in a critical condition. I decided to work with a tape, and with participants' permission, to record our conversations. These ranged around their perceptions of the hospice, and their feelings about their illness and death. I gathered stories, documented work lives and recorded events.

I would read the transcription of the tape back to the participant, often to their delight and surprise. They would then add or edit, until they were happy with their piece. Again with prior agreement, a copy of each piece was posted up on a noticeboard along a corridor approaching the ward.

In transcribing a tape, I would sometimes change the order in which things were said, but never the way in which they were said.

Each participant decided for themselves what they wanted to change when they saw their words written down. The pieces trace the rhythms of speech, the choice of vocabulary and turn of phrase of patients, providing a record in which patients took pride, and which relatives and friends valued. One piece was read out at a patient's funeral. Others have been sent to friends and relatives in different parts of the country and abroad.

Many people involved in the hospice have similar motivation – personal experience of terminal illness. It didn't seem appropriate to separate off patients and relatives from other groups in the hospice. I therefore included volunteers and staff in the process of interviewing. This lack of segregation is reflected in the sequencing of the book.

Many of the patients, volunteers and staff come up against fear and prejudice about staying in or working in a hospice. In compiling this book I hope to allay some of those fears, and to increase awareness about the quality of life which a hospice can help provide. Creativity can play an integral part in that quality.

Occasionally a participant would talk about a patient who had died before I was able to work with them. Brenda Kenyon talks about Molly Saville, and Cora Margerison talks about Pat Holt. Margaret Macdonald talks about her husband Billy when he had become too ill to work with me.

My thanks to all at Springhill Hospice who have gave me generous quantities of their time, wisdom, comfort, support and wit, especially Kay Scott. Thank-you also for the kindness and indulgence of Suzannah Dunn, Christine Bridgewood, Mog Ball, Myna Trustram, Rosie Gleeson, Kevin Fegan, Tony Ward and John Killick.

Chrissie Gittins
Writer-in-Residence, Springhill Hospice

Springhill Hospice.

1 Brenda Kenyon

My first experience of coming into here was with a little apprehension, of course. I didn't really know what I was coming into, a completely new environment. But I have been so overwhelmed at the treatment, and the help, support, that I've had since I've been in.

The hospice itself is, really only one word to describe it, is beautiful. The surrounding area is fields, horses around, lots of birdlife, which is a pleasure to look out on. Each bed has a view through the windows.

The nurses are really just absolutely great. They can't do enough for you. You feel sometimes that you might be mithering, but nothing is too much trouble for them.

It's nice that the ministers — the priests come in on a regular basis — treat you all the same, which I feel that they should do. They're so easy to talk to. They come in so unassuming, and they don't outstay their welcome. Sometimes I find that one or two of them can do, and you get stuck for words, particularly if it's a minister not of your faith.

I've had my eyes opened to a different side of nursing. I've been in various hospitals. I have been in Christie's twice, and the nursing there has been absolutely fantastic. But I do realize that the hospice is not giving you the nursing facilities that the big hospitals give you. They are here more to care for the pain and more for the terminally ill people. Even though at the moment, touching wood, I don't feel that I am a terminally ill patient, they have helped me tremendously to think more positively. But I do feel that I do think very very positively. A lot of people have said to me that that has helped to pull me through a long long way.

I have wanted to think positively, because I've got a marvellous supportive family, a very close family, and I want to live. I feel I'm not ready for another world. And this is the only way I can look at it. I must think positively. Alright, the nurses here are inclined to say to you, live a day at a time. But, yes, I am living a day at a time, but I'm also thinking of the months ahead, not just the days. For the months ahead, and what's going to happen this summer, not just to-day. We are tentatively making holiday arrangements, but, I said to Jim last night, my husband, "Do you think we are perhaps being a bit too rushing, Jim." He said, "No, we're doing what we normally do."

It is a problem, and it's a problem that sometimes you want to push to the back of your mind. Many many times, and I wonder if it is the right thing to do, I want to forget. I go to bed some nights, and I think, "I'm going to be much better tomorrow morning." Perhaps tomorrow morning I *am* better. Perhaps I'm not quite as good as I was the day before, but I'm going to fight that day. And that day might work out a little bit easier than the day before.

I haven't found it easy to come to terms with. I find sometimes that I've been cheated. And I'm sure that a lot of other ladies and gentlemen must feel the same. Very aggressive, – the way that life has suddenly turned on you. Maybe in my case, having brought up a family, and we were now both beginning to feel that life was getting easier for us. The family had grown up, and I get landed now with not being able to get out and about like we would have loved to have done. This is where I get very upset sometimes. I feel life has passed me by a little. But it can't be a bed of roses for everybody. Some have to take the rough with the smooth.

*

I have worked for doctors. I worked for five years for a practice in my locality. I enjoyed that work very very much. Over the last seven years I've worked for social services in Manchester, working for the social workers who were dealing with adoption and fostering. I found that very very rewarding, very distressing, but a lot of pleasurable moments.

I've seen small children being taken from their mothers at birth, because the mothers have not been able to care for them. They'd been abused themselves, and we have to avoid their children being abused. But then I've had the pleasure of seeing their new adoptive parents taking them away, for the first time, and realizing how lucky those children were to be going to a new home, and a home that they would be wanted in. And that to me is so rewarding. I've had a lot of pleasurable times seeing that. And that is the lovely moments of life really. And it really is. You can forget a lot of your problems, when you think of those happy moments. I miss not being able to go to work to see those moments and carry them further. But I've had a lot of pleasure from it, very much so.

*

Molly (Saville) was one of life's very genuine humble, people, I feel. I think she'd had quite a hard life, I didn't get to know her very well, because I was only with her for about a week. But she was always laughing and joking, and she got on very well with everybody. She wasn't ashamed to say what she wanted. One day, she'd have a little swear, but it was all in the fun of the day. One particular afternoon she had four visitors, and they were laughing and joking, and they were having a whale of a time. However lovely it was to hear her, being able to be jolly, her natural self, with these friends that she evidently has been friends with for many many years, who live in the same street as she did.

She was a very devoted mother, a mother who she said had kept her family together. She had a daughter and a son, and four grandchildren. And they all seemed to think the world of her, and as she said, she'd kept her family close together. Her words were as she went out, "Well, I've left my mark here."

One of her highlights, a week last Sunday, we went to the church service, and it was the Bishop of Salford, who came to preach. And it's only a small chapel, and Molly wasn't a catholic, I'm not a catholic, but we went, and we thoroughly enjoyed the service. She came back to her bed afterwards, and Dr Robert Gartside, the General Practitioner from here, came to Molly, and asked her, would she come back and have her photograph taken. And she was so over the moon that they'd asked her to come back and have her photograph taken with the bishop. And she said, "Me not even dressed properly, and not a catholic."

*

Having been in here for two weeks, I have a little knowledge of how the hospice is run, and I find it rather upsetting that the hospice is not being utilized to the full. I feel that there must be many many people that would benefit from being in a place like this. It is a purpose built place, and I would like to see, which ever way possible, that it could be utilized.

I know it's lack of funds but I would wish and hope, soon, something can be done to improve the situation, because it must, otherwise, what was the point of all this being built, and all the hard work and effort?

I admire everybody who works here, the volunteer workers, and the nursing staff, I can do nothing but praise. I have enjoyed the stay tremendously. I go home with glowing colours. The friends that have been here to see me, and I've had plenty of friends, they have all been absolutely over the moon with what they have seen. So much so, I feel that the hospice, hopefully, might benefit from my friends.

2   Tommy Dutton

Now I'm retired, it's my life, as you might call it. You know I'm up here every day. I think, for the people that come in here, they meet another smiling face, as you might say. Being in charge of this, the shop, you meet that many different people. I do nothing else only this now, each day, other than Thursdays. Well, it's like I say, I look forward to it, I do.

To me, it's a marvellous place. And the staff, they're like a family really. They treat every patient, and I nearly see them all coming in. Quite a good few do go out an' all. It's a new place and I've never heard a wrong word about it. Almost off anybody. I was coming in here almost before it was finished. When my daughter found out she'd got the matron, I was all for it, helping in my way, kind of style. But I can't praise it enough. The nurses are a grand crowd.

We started off with a few items of chocolate and a few drinks. But, from that, people have got to know, and word's got round that you don't need to carry stuff up there, you can buy it in the shop. We haven't a lot of space, but we do have a variety.

The Hospice shop.

3 Ted Worthington

We got married, and we were both more or less orphans. The wife, her mother and father died when they were in their thirties. He had a job in the mill which was a killer. He did what they call stripping and grinding in the card room. The cards had all spikes, and they pull the cotton to pieces. Well, they have to be clean, and they used to have to go underneath, brush it out, and it gets on the chest. He was only thirty-odd, tubercular. Her Mum, worked on the trams during the 1914 to 1919 war. When she was driving the trams, they had a trick of swinging the brake handle round. It was on a spring. It sprung back and caught her, and hit her on the breast. Then she was at a cricket match. She got hit on the breast with a cricket ball. After that she had to have the breast taken off, it killed her. That was her mother and father.

My dad died of cancer, when he was forty-four, or something like that. My mum was ailing when he died, and she died of bronchial trouble.

I was doing a bit of courting at the time, I was about eighteen. She was in service, so we decided, well, we might as well get married. We got married, and I was just turned nineteen. Since then, we've had two boys and two girls.

There are more opportunities now than they had, otherwise, in my day, they'd have just stayed put. I remember when they used to go working half time. There were that many cotton mills round here, they couldn't get the employees, so they used to have youngsters going from school at twelve years old, working in the cotton. They'd do a morning in the mill, start at six, then the week after they'd do an afternoon, in the cotton. And they'd go to school in between. This was in the twenties. I don't remember any good old days. Yet, there were happy days. People were more in a unit. Not like now, you go and live in a place and you don't know your next door neighbour. In those days they were like all little villages together, even in a town. Just knock on the door, or put the latch down and walk in. They always helped.

I was a heating engineer. I worked for Ferranti's. They were a family firm, and you got treated more or less as part of the family. I joined the Navy for three years, in 1942, which was a big change in my life. The workpeople at Ferranti's started a fund, home comforts for the men in the services. Which meant you got such things a mittens, scarves, balaclavas, socks. You used to get a small parcel every month out of the comforts fund. Plus, the firm themselves donated so much for each child and so much for the wife. Which was a great help because things were a bit dicey in those days. When you came on leave, they always told you you had to report into the personnel department, and there was always some more comforts fund there, which was great. Nothing but praise for Ferranti's.

That period in the Navy till 1945, I think it taught me to appreciate home life more. That was one thing, you were always glad when you did get leave to go home to the wife and the family. I'd no regrets, because I volunteered. I had some good times and some bad times. It soon passed. Then going back to Civvy Street, without any trouble, adapting to the usual way of life, which had changed quite a lot even in those days. That was one of the milestones in my life.

*

When I came to the hospice, I didn't know what to expect, because people get a false impression of what it is like. They expect everybody to be carried out ready for the boneyard. I was really surprised. From the first day I stepped in, it seemed as though I was stepping in, like a balloon. Separate from the rest of the world, floating. Everything changes ever so peaceful. You feel better right away, before you've even got to your room. That's how I felt anyway. From that day, to now, I've improved every day, through some unknown reason. Everything's five star hotel treatment.

Anything that you really ask for, they'll find it for you, one way or another. All the amusement you want, all the tape-recorders and what have you. There are about eight of us now, but I think if it got to full, the staff would be run off their feet, to cater as they are doing now, for the patients. And Matron's superb. Matron's superb.

I could've had a single room. I didn't fancy talking to myself like, so I got the next room. It's been smashing with Roy. We help one another. I've just left him now, I said, "It'll be your turn next to go down to the village."

Everybody's so nice, loving. It's a lovely feeling. Two strangers just come in now and they were asking what it's like. First day I came in here changed my life altogether, very pleased to say. Just been out now, I've been in here a week, and I feel ready for going home, and I'm not quite fit yet. Been down in the village, a little pub there, just had an hour away. The lady what just does it one day a week, very nice, person, Cora. She takes you down to the pub, but she's teetotal.

The last time I went in that pub was in 1943 when I was in the Navy. Funnily enough, when I got in, I could remember where I sat, and who I sat with. There were four of us, all men. One was a school mate of mine, he was in the airforce, two were in the army. We'd all been young people together. It was a nice trip out. And I'm looking forward to another, week from to-day. I should be going out, I'm sure of that. It gives you that feeling, where you come in with no hope.

I'd like to thank my wife. We've had happy days me and the wife. She's been a gem. As ill as I am, she's kept going. And the daughter. She's looked after us both.

4   Ann Howson

It's a lovely place to work. It's a good atmosphere amongst the staff. We're all quite different, but we've gelled as a team. Personally, I feel it's an honour to come into work, and look after some of these patients. You think you've got your problems and your moans and your groans, but they put everything in perspective for you.

It's a lot different from where I worked before because I was on a busy surgical ward. And I found the transition from running round and always being busy, to coming and spending more time with your patients, not having to rush round if they wanted to lie in the bath for half an hour – I found that difficult. I kept thinking, "Oh my God, I've got this to do, I've got that to do." But, I've slowed down now.

It is very different from a general hospital. On admission, we don't do temperatures, pulses, respiration, blood pressure. We sit and interview the patients and the family, or main carer, be it husband, wife, daughter, son, to get to know what they've been through with their illness, what they feel are the problems. It gives us a picture to be able to make our aims and objectives for caring for them. We involve the relatives in the care, which is lovely. It's none of this 'Excuse me, will you leave the room?' If they want to help us turn them, or put them in the bath, they're more than welcome. I find that nice, working alongside the relatives. I always thought I was pushing them out in a hospital. You know, it wasn't their Mum, it wasn't their Dad, we'd taken them off them when they came in. They are part of the care here, which I like.

I always interview a relative without the patient, if I can. You tend to get two different stories when you interview them differently. The patient will be trying to be brave and cover up for the relative, and vice versa. But if you get them on their own, they're more open. I also find it gives the relative a chance to open up and have a damn good cry if that's what they want. I think a lot of it's relief, because you're honest with them, and you're open and it's all up front. But, I think that makes a better relationship, you bond better with them there and then.

*

We had a gentleman in, not too very long ago, and he got a little bit aggressive towards the nursing staff, but he was confused. And he was adamant that he was going home, and he wanted to be at home. And we're not a prison. If he wants to be at home and spend his last days there, then, that's where he should be. But the day before he went home he put his false teeth in a papier mâchée urinal, which was placed in the bedpan machine and chewed up. One of our senior members of staff had to explain it on the 'phone to his wife. There's no easy way of saying he's got no teeth left.

*

It's like an extension of my family. It's the happiest place I've ever worked.

5 Bill Wheeler

This began in the fifties, where Anthony Nutting, who was involved in the Anthony Eden government, was out in Cairo, talking to Colonel Nasser, prior to the Suez invasion. He came back, and promised Nasser there would be a hold on any invasion of Egypt. He said there would be a hold for twenty-four hours, and he would let him know the reply of the Prime Minister. But on his way back, he actually passed an invasion force of allied aircraft. Whilst he was away, Ben Gurion, who was the Prime Minister of Israel, Mulli, the Prime Minister of France, and Anthony Eden, had colluded together and gone out and invaded Suez. Anthony Nutting resigned.

As a matter of fact, he was called into the Prime Minister's office.

The way the Tories used to do it in them days, they used to pass on the premiership, there was no elections. And he was actually offered, on Anthony Eden's resignation, the premiership. He offered him the premiership, if he would keep his mouth shut over what had happened. He knew his political career was in shreds because of what he'd done, because he'd no mandate to do it. Anthony Nutting said no, that he wouldn't do this, and he resigned from politics.

Some years later, sixty-three, sixty-four, he came to Oldham to try and get back into politics. I went to a meeting. Possibly because of the personality, I knew him as Anthony Nutting, and I'd read his book, "Lawrence of Arabia," I was sat there, and probably was the only socialist in the place. They were all old ladies asking about was there going to be a raising in pensions, and general run of the mill questions. He spoke with an Oxbridge University accent. I stood and said, it was alright him coming from his ivory towers in London, i.e. Cheyne Walk, and how could he begin to understand the working classes of a cotton town like Oldham? Which was quite derelict in those days, they were knocking houses down all over the place. He came down to me after the meeting and he said, you show me around Oldham.

We arranged a night to show him round Oldham. They were knocking an area down in Oldham which was absolutely diabolical, it was called West Street. It was a biggish area, and in this particular street, I'd noted that there were eight houses which were still to be knocked down with people living in them. At the back of the house where they'd had back yards, they'd knocked the yards down to get the vehicles in for when they eventually decided to pull the building down. And there were just two toilets, you see.

So, of course, the first place I went was to this West Street. I said, "Now look," I said, "there's eight houses there, now let's go round the back. There's just two toilets," I said, "and they all want to go to the toilet. And the Labour Party, in its history, has only been in power for thirteen years. So all the ills of this town cannot be blamed on the Labour Party." And then I took him into a pub, called 'The Turn of Luck,' and it was a real dump. It had sawdust on the floor, and this is in the sixties, it sounds as if it was in the thirties.

Come the election day, I didn't vote for him, I voted for Charles Map, the sitting member. I went to the count, just out of interest. I thought that he may have pulled it off, because he was very popular, and he spoke very well. And he was definitely better educated than what Charles Map were. Charles Map was an ex-railway man, who'd gone probably through the unions. Anyway, he lost. He came to me and give a me a dig in the ribs, and he said, "You can't win them all, can you Bill?" And he said, "Had you voted for me, I wouldn't have wanted to know you." I said, "I know you wouldn't." There was a glow between us.

He went home, and within a couple of days I got this letter. Quite a brief one, but a nice one, saying that whilst we were political enemies, he felt sure that we'd become personal friends. And he invited me to come and stay in his ivory tower in Cheyne Walk. Then I got a telegram from him, and he put on the telegram, pre-paid telegram by the way, "Acquired ringside seats, Cassius Clay – Henry Cooper fight. Will you travel?" So I just put on, "Bravo, will travel." So, I told my Dad, who was a good old socialist, and he said, "You're crackers, lad." He said, "This fella'll have a butler, you know, and servants." I said, "Will he heck, Dad. Don't talk ridiculous."

I went out and I spent thirty-five pounds on a suit, which was an astronomical amount of money. I had a bath in the morning, and I went to London. I got to the station in London, and I felt right toffee-nosed myself saying number seven Cheyne Walk please. The driver dropped me off, and this is when I started to get butterflies.

I saw the place, and I went and either rang the bell, or knocked on the knocker, I don't remember which, and the butler came to the door. And he said, "Mr Wheeler, Sir?" I can hear him now, and I nearly died, you know. Anyway, I went in, and Tony met me, and Anne, his wife. Before I knew where I was I had a Bloody Mary in my hand. I didn't know what it was, but they said, would you like a bloody Mary. I was there with this wacking great big, like a brandy bowl, but bigger.

I was very nervous, very nervous indeed when I saw inside. Beautiful furnishings, old worldy type furnishings, but very very very beautiful, and very expensive indeed. I'd been there, possibly half an hour, and beginning to relax, and the butler came through to me, and I'll never forget this as long as I live, and he said to me, "Would you like a bath, sir?" I thought, well, it must be the done thing in these circles, to have another bath when you've travelled, so I said, "Yes, I would like a bath, please." He said, "How would you like your water, sir?" I hadn't a clue how to answer, I said, "I'll have it normal."

The day went by, Friday evening arrived, and Tony said, "I've a treat in store, there's a car picking us up." So, we went and got us ready, just the two of us. We gets in this chauffer driven car, and we picked up David Niven. Tony introduced me, he said, "This is the bugger that kept me out of parliament, Nivvie. This is Bill." I said, "Hello, Mr Niven, pleased to meet you." He said, "Nivvie," I said, "Oh, right, Nivvie." Then we went and picked up another man, he was an osteopath in Harley Street.

I was associated with the youth club at the time, and I wanted to get some programmes. So, I said to Tony, we were sat at the end of the row, "When he comes past, can you get me half a dozen programmes?" He said, "Certainly I can." He gives me these programmes, I said, "What do I owe you?" He said, "Oh, forget it." I looked at them, they're a quid a piece. I said, "No, I insist that you have this money." He said, "Bill, I will smack your hands and face," he said, "This week-end, you don't spend a penny," and I didn't, literally, apart from the gent's toilets. I spent half a crown, tipping the fella. When I was washing my hands he brushed my shoulders. They threw half a crown in this little saucer, and I had to throw in half a crown, which I thought was rather expensive.

We finished up, we came out, and we got on the carpark, and we couldn't get off the carpark. We stood there for ages, and Ronnie, David Niven's chauffer, he said to him, "Ronnie, I think you'd better go and get us some bottles, because we're going to be sat here for quite a long while. The pair of them, by the way, in comparison to me were scruffily dressed, they hadn't dressed up at all, you see, where I had. He came back with these bottles and they were literally knocking the top of the bottles off on what you shut the door with. I just couldn't believe this at all that I was sat with David Niven, this osteopath and Tony Nutting, drinking bottles.

On another occasion, he simply said, we're going out to lunch. We walked into this restaurant in King's Road, I marches in, I said, "Look who's there, I'm sure that's King Faisal." He said, "You're showing your ignorance, William," he said, "it's King Hussein," and before I knew where I was, he was introducing me to him and we were sitting down having lunch. He's very quietly spoken and you had to really listen to hear what he said. He talks very very slowly, and you know what he's going to say before he says it. I find his situation very very sad at the moment.

I came home, and I marches in the house, and I'm talking to my wife, she says to me, "You're talking posh." I realized that I was. What I'd done, he'd invited his family down, for Sunday lunch. I became aware that I'd a Lancashire accent. Everything was done proper, it was wheeled in, tureens were put out, the staff put out what they put out and he carved the meat. I became aware that I'd a Lancashire accent and I started to sound my aitches, and brought it home with me.

*

The friendship has gone on all through the years, and up to the present date. We've always communicated with each other. I think it was my wife who let him know that I was poorly. He came on the 'phone and said, how are you like. I said, O.K.. I hadn't had my operation then. When I'd had my operation, I got flowers sent in the hospital and he wrote to me. Then I went on the 'phone. I thought I'd only a limited amount of time left to live. I wanted to thank him really for his friendship.

I remember saying to him that although we came from poles apart — and he's a baron now, it's Right Honourable Sir Anthony Nutting, Bart. — that our friendship had transcended the barriers between his type of life and the working class background that I came from. I was in tears when I was saying this. The next thing I could hear is this man crying down the other end of the 'phone. He said to me, "William, William, William. He said, let's try and stop crying. This is heartbreaking news. But," he said, "You're going to come to London, we're going to go out, and we're going to dine in the finest place in London. We're going to have the finest Claret. We've got to do this William. If only once. We've got to meet each other again." I said to him, because I was very despondent, I said, "I doubt if I can get to London, Tony." I think, we both finished up really cried up and said cheerio to each other. I think we both had to put the 'phone down.

He possibly now rings me once a fortnight, or I ring him. We just have a jolly good old natter on the 'phone, and every time he comes on, he just says, "Are you coming down?" I don't feel fit enough to go. I've no doubt he would come here if I said, come up here. But I'm a little reticent, I haven't a scruffy house, but I'm a little reticent with the fact that he has such a beautiful house, to bring him down to mine. And it wouldn't make the slightest bit of difference to him. It wouldn't make the slightest bit of difference.

I think my father was proud really, in a funny sort of a way, that our Bill could go and stay with him. And it's been a dear friendship, and a deep friendship. Although we don't see each other very often, when we do, there's a lot of affection between us. And it's been as much from him.

6 Beatrice Marriott and Irene Hilton

Beatrice
There is only two of us what cleans the whole hospice really. The volunteers do whatever they can. We try to keep on top of everything, not just the vacuuming, the dusting, and the wiping down, it's all underneath the beds we go. And any of the nurses, you know, have you got time to help us make a bed?, we'll drop our tools and do it.

You work at one hospital, as a domestic, and the nursing staff are on a different side to you altogether. Here, no. Nobody tells you, will you do this, and will you do that? If there's anything at all to be done, would you mind doing it?

Some patients you can get very close to. And then when they do die you do get upset. But you do know that they are being looked after, very well. I only wish it had been open when my Mum was dying of cancer. But there wasn't such a place.

Irene
We'll have a go at anything, nursing, talk to the relations. I think people give vibes, you know, if they don't want to talk.

I've been a domestic all my working life. I've worked in a school and a hospital, mainly a school. I stuck at it, because it's money, isn't it, at the end of the day. At the infirmary I worked on casualty. If you went in the staffroom to clean, they'd go out. But here, it's not like that, everybody's the same. You don't feel somewhere on the floor.

Hanging tea bags on a line? Because it were charity, you know, they needed all the pennies that they could. And they were saving tea bags and re-using them. So, Marylyn left a note, would I peg them up? And like an idiot I did.

7 Stanley Wyers

In the old metal days of the printing industry, the type, where each letter was a separate piece of metal, fitted into a tray with the whole alphabet and figures, each one in its own separate little box. The ones that you used most were closest to hand in the middle of the case.

We used to do a boring job, the apprentices, a boring job, called diss. Which is putting away old words that's been finished with. The work was broken up, and each letter was put back into its own box in the case that it came from. Different sizes of type went in different cases.

I was dissing one day in a large case, with a lot of very small type in it, and I must have caught the case with my elbow, and the case slid gently off the frame on which it was placed, turned over, and fell on the floor. Emptied the entire contents of the case into one big heap on the floor. It took me two days to pick it all up and distribute it back into the case into its right boxes.

I worked all over the country to some extent. We moved from the North West, to the South East in the early fifties, and I worked for what is known as a provincial newspaper down there, called the Hertfordshire Express.

The national newspaper industry is highly unionised, or was, the unions were very strong. And they resisted change for quite a number of years. Eventually, for economic reasons, it was virtually forced upon them. In the last seven years, it's been a gradual changeover in the national newspaper industry to computerised typesetting, where no metal is used at all hardly, until the very final stages, where a plate is used which fits on a rotary printing machine. It's much quieter, much cleaner, and generally a more efficient method of printing. And instead of being highly skilled people, as in hot metal, the computer keyboard is very similar to a typewriter keyboard. A lot of the work can be done by semi-trained people. They don't have to serve long apprenticeships.

At the end of 1985, the newspaper I was working for at that time, went new technology. The age at which you could be re-trained was fixed at the age of about forty-five. And if you were older than forty-five, you were considered too old for re-training. It was too expensive to spend that capital on a man who only had, say, fifteen or twenty years' working life left in him.

I can imagine to-day will be a very hectic day in the newspaper business. The office where I used to work, it'll be like a snowstorm. There'll be copy being changed every hour. With the Prime Minister resigning, the story is added to as the day goes along, as developments occur. There'll be speculation as to who is going to succeed her as leader of the Conservative Party.

And of course, it doesn't fall that whoever wins the leadership is going to be Prime Minister, because that's not the way the constitution works. The way the constitution works, if she's resigning as Prime Minister, she has to tender her resignation to the Queen. And then the Queen has to decide if whoever succeeds her as leader of the Conservative Party is strong enough to form a government among a party that's already in disarray. She could quite easily ask Neil Kinnock to come along and form a minority government. In which case it's almost certain, as I've seen things in the past like this, it's almost certain he would call a general election immediately.

In the newspaper industry, they'll be jamming their stories in all the time. And they update as the day and the night goes along, right through the night, it doesn't stop.

8   Betty Portman

Margaret said to me in the bungalow one evening, could we start a hospice? And I said, what a great idea. We were in the Red Cross together, and bearing in mind we both lost our husbands with cancer, within six months of one another, an identical tumour, this is where the common ground came in. The next time I saw her, I said, just a minute, let's think about what we're going to do. She said, you're too late, I've started. But we took off from there.

I don't think we realised at that stage what we would have to do. We sat and we thought about it all – no money. What are we going to do? Right, we'll buy football cards, and we'll sell them to everyone we can think of. The winnner had half, and we had half. And that gave us some money to do our publicity. That was in February 1983, and on May 10th we launched a public appeal. We went to St. Chad's in Rochdale, more naive than I ever thought. We went to Middleton and we launched there, and then we launched in Heywood, told people what we thought we would do. Suddenly support groups started, Wardle started one, Rochdale started one, Milnrow started one, Heywood had one. And it seemed to snowball from there. We did all sorts of silly things to make money.

We had a brochure printed to publicize the appeal. The plans were on the architect's wall in the Health Authority. The local builder went into the office and he said, "What's that?" pointing to the plans. The architect said, "It's a hospice for Rochdale that I'm designing." The builder said, "Funny really, I read it in the 'Architect' recently that McAlpine were building a Windsor hospice, so I'm interested in that." He went away and rang Arthur Potts, the architect, the next day, and said, "I will build this hospice at cost. If a firm in the South can build a hospice at cost, we can do it better in the North." It was on a plate, wasn't it?

But it still wasn't easy, we still needed money. Oh God, we did parachute jumps, Krypton Factors, you name it, we did it. Everything that was possible to raise money, just everything. In the January Sales we went round the Sales and we bought all sorts of stuff that would do for tombolas and prizes.

We met with Arthur, the architect, and his team, and we said we want this building built, and we want the best building that you ever designed. We then went and got permission from the hospices in the North West, and we covered everybody. And we went to have a look at their hospices, and said what would you do now if you had the chance to alter things, what did you do wrong? We got a load of information, gave it to the architect and said, this is what we want, this is what we've chosen. Will you go out and see these buildings and see what you can do for us. That's what he came up with. he came up with the design, then the builder appeared, as if by magic.

We had to furnish it then, didn't we? That was a very hard task. The design team liased with Kay. We didn't have anything to do with it then, it was up to Matron then, we said, it's yours. We'd done what we said we would do.

Then, of course, the shop came into being. This is the main fundraising thing. We had a shop down the street, it was to be for rent, but Margaret went to the council and said, "Can we have it free?" We got it free. And then, of course, they started building the Wheatsheaf and we had to come out, and we had nowhere to go. This was the only building the council owned on the street. So cap in hand again, we went to the council, and they said we can have this shop. It was in a terrible state. Looking back, we must have been crackers. We were closed twelve months from this shop to that shop.

A very good band of voluntary workers, without whom we couldn't manage. Every day downstairs the staff changes. Up here it's the same people all the time. And, they really are, I don't know anyone else who would work like they do for nothing. They say they don't get paid for anything here, but you do get free coffee, she gives you that. It's altered, it's washed, dried, ironed. And what we can't sell, the ragman buys off us.

Even my grandchildren are now hospice-minded. That'll do for grandma's hospice.

9   Denis Norminton

I worked for Oldham Council as a road sweeper for nine years. I enjoyed the job very much, till this problem came along. It was one of those jobs where when you got up of a morning you enjoyed getting up to go to work. Weird as that may sound that was how you felt.

During the winter months while we were on gritting, people followed us on motorbikes hoping that we'll go right to their house to get them home safely.

One old gentleman, early hours of one morning, about five o'clock in the morning, thought we was going to go right through to Yorkshire to grit. And he found out we turned round at the border. He had a think about it for about five minutes, then when I looked in the mirrors again to see where he was, he was right behind me coming down the hill. I mean he must have been in agony with the amount of salt we were throwing out behind us. He must have had a good pasting with the salt. He didn't expect to get the weather he met up on the Holmfirth Road. Which not a lot of people does. He'd have to wait for another gritting crew coming from the Yorkshire side. It may have been another hour.

*

Well, what can you say about it? It's an unbelievable place. Anything you want, they're there for you. They don't allow you to have any pain whatsoever. All you do is you press the button. Somebody's there. It's no problem whatsoever. Superbly run, the meals are fantastic, everything.

They don't hide anything. Whatever you want to know, you ask, they'll tell you. That is a brilliant thing. At least you know where you stand. Which has got to be a good thing. Because you don't want to be told one thing and knowing another thing is going to happen. You've got to have the truth in these places.

10   Cora Margerison

Even before it were built, years ago, I'm going back eight or nine year now, I've always done the Rochdale fun run for the hospice. And then, eight year ago, my mum died of cancer. There were no

View across the quadrangle.

hospices around to take her anywhere, and we didn't have transport or anything. We had to go to Christie's. And I thought it's a good idea to have one.

I've been involved from day one since it opened, when we had to go to interview. You're intereviewed as a volunteer. You have four sides of paper to fill in, and two referees. Like having a full time job.

I work in the kitchen, take patients their brews, and take patients for a walk, to the pub. They love it you know, honestly. It's just a shame there's not more volunteers to take more patients out for a long walk. I never hear of a lot of people doing it. I know everybody's busy in here, but you've just got to make a bit of time. Like a patient to-day asked me, she said, I'd love to go for a walk, I've always gone for a walk. I said, "I'll take you." She's dead chuffed.

I just enjoy it every time I come here.

A week last Tuesday I took a patient out for a walk, took her to the pub. She bought me a coke and blackcurrant, and she had a rum and coke. The pub has a coal fire. She seemed right as rain, she was on about going home, and she were really going to get herself going. She said it would help if she had a lift in the house. She worked in a bank, and had three children.

And no way did I think that patient was going to die. In fact, I said to Pat (Holt), we'll come back next week. We said to the landlady of the pub, we'll see you next week. I come the following Monday for the volunteers buffet, and I was going to have a talk with her for ten minutes. I asked one of the nurses where were Pat, and she said she'd died.

That night I were really upset. Two of the nurses yesterday come up to me, and there were one nurse who'd been with Pat when she died, and she said how she really enjoyed the walk out and going to the pub.

*

The kitchen which I am in, and like there's two girls on one week and then two girls another week, they do alternate weeks, are great and always have been. And the volunteers I work with are great. In fact I just think everybody's wonderful.

I never ever read a book. The only thing I read is Wednesday's (Rochdale) *Observer* and Saturday's *Observer*. Nothing else, because I don't like reading. But if a book was printed about the hospice I would buy it and I would read it.

I am the chief cook in the kitchen and I wear a cook's hat. All the patients comment and like my hat. On my hat, it says, "Dieting is for the birds." It has a green band. One patient said to me once, she touched it like this, she said, "You've got some grass on your head."

11   Elaine Harling and Gladys Storey

Elaine

I rang up and I come for an interview and I got the job. It was about three month before getting the job to it opening, so I had three month to think about it. I tossed and turned it over in my mind, for three month, whether to come or not. Thoughts of working with terminally ill people, I didn't know if I could handle or not. But I think I've handled it quite well.

I think the thing I was frightened of more than anything, I was frightened of seeing a dead body. It really frightened me did that. Dr Bob took me to see my first one and I can go and look at anybody now. We get attached to some of them, and I'll go and see them and have a little chat.

Like Amelia, who's just died, I used to work with Amelia thirty year ago. So, it was nice seeing her. I went to see her when she'd died. I don't go and see them all. The ones that I get attached to.

I think at first when we used to prepare these meals, and serve them up and they were all left, you used to think, "God, perhaps they didn't like them." I'd only ever cooked for schoolchildren before. But, you come to realize, that they just can't stomach it some of the time.

One patient that comes to mind — we used to go down in a morning and ask the patients what they wanted for breakfast. We used to wake Nelly up every morning, "What would you like for your breakfast?" She used to wake up really pleasant every morning. She'd say, "All I'd like really, is a fag." She loved going having her hair done, and her nails. She'd come out with a beam from here to here. She thought she was in the Hilton Hotel. She came in before Christmas, and she wanted to stay till Mother's Day. She didn't want to go home at all.

Gladys

I retired from school meals after eighteen years and I thought that was it. Then one of the girls said this job was coming up, and I thought I'm too old, you know. The night I came, for just the form to fill in, the queue, I thought, I've no chance. But they all came for different jobs, they weren't just for the kitchen. And as it happened, you see, it's life in the old dog yet.

When I asked the headmaster for a reference, he said, "Why do you want to go there?" So I said, "Well, I've enjoyed working with children, one end of the line, so I'm going to work with the other, the old ones."

I quite enjoy coming, it's not like coming to work really. With the week on, the week off, that breaks it up. I quite enjoy coming.

If you can get these patients to eat, it's a bonus isn't it? Half of them when they come in they haven't eaten for a month or so, six weeks, something like that.

I remember when I first came, though, I was coming down the corridor, and there was the three side wards, with patients in them, sat up, eating bacon and egg. We had cooked it, so we knew. I came past, I looked, and I thought, "Well, I couldn't eat bacon and egg this time in the morning." It seemed funny for these poorly people to be having a cooked breakfast.

It makes you feel good when you think, well, they haven't been eating and then they come in here and ...

Me and Elaine get on alright. I mean, if you're happy at your work it's everything, isn't it? And it's not a miserable place at all. It's not like somewhere to come for the end, is it?

12 Mary Redmond

My Mum got married and she had ten children. I was born in 1915, so therefore I was born during the war. And I was born the date that my father landed in Gallipoli. Very funny that.

Most of us were born on the end of Milnrow Road. We lived there until we were teenagers because our mother died when she were only forty-nine. And left them all. David got married, but Henry were at home, Lizzie were at home, the twins were at home, Bill and Harriet, my sister Nan were at home, I was at home, George were at home, Jack were at home. We all lived together there. But my father were there. My father used to go in the Odd Fellows having a drink.

It was very funny living there all by yourself with nobody superintending. One good thing was us all being in the house on Friday night waiting for the rent man. It was old Birtwell that used to come. He were a cripple with a stick. And he used to come and shout out "Rent." And we all used to turn round and say, "Spent." Till at finish he got fed up of us. We had to find other accommodation.

One of my twin brothers, he was a sodpot. Him and his mate were drunk one day, cleaning the windows. One were inside and one were outside, can you imagine?

Our Bill had a bird on his arm, one of them they print on. Especially if my girlfriends were in or my sister's girlfriends were in, he used to say, "Well, I'll have to wash my bird now." They used to get up and fly out, in case they didn't understand exactly what this bird were. Because there were no bathrooms then you see. Everybody washed in the sink.

We used to have to go all the way round Milnrow Road, through the entry to the toilet at the back. Nearly everybody shared them, because there weren't enough toilets for everyone to have one, so different families shared the same one. You'd be queueing up, especially when you'd a fella there that would chew his tobacco, and sit on the toilet. Used to go round the back and have a look at his arse. They had to have a hole at the back to drag the tubs out.

With the Depression that came on in the thirties, you had to put on the Labour School, if you wanted to get your dole. But the only thing they taught you was, "My Bonny Lies Over the Ocean." I got fed up of that, so I left and I went in private service in a public. I looked after the woman's two children while they run the pub.

The landlord, Harry, Harry had a night out one night with different landlords from different public houses. Some anniversary of somert it were. Did you know Diggles and Taylor's that used to be in Taylor street, a place that used to have men's only second hand gear? Well, he was so drunk, him and his mates fell in it. Halfway up the stairs in the public, they had the Cherry Boy, you know that statue, with the Cherry Boy sat down with his basket and his cherries. I was wiping the window bottoms half way up and this Cherry Boy was sat there. Half way up the stairs of course, he'd put his arm out to steady himself and knocked the Cherry Boy off on the tiles.

I was up first in the morning, which I always used to be, because I used to tidy up and that before they got up. When I got up, I thought to myself, "Good God! He were alright last night." So, I picked the biggest pieces up and swept the other up out of the way. It'd be about eight o'clock, something like that, the police came. "Harry Homes live here? Can I see him?" I said, "I'm sorry, you can't, he's gone out." He said, "What at this time at morning after what he did last night?" I said, "Why, what did he do last night?" He said, "We want him because he put a window through." I said, "I don't think it were Harry. Because he's out now. If he were drunk last night, he wouldn't be out this time in a morning." So they said, "We'll come back." So I went and woke him up and put him right. I said, "You'd better piss off out and crack on you've only just come in."

I stayed with them until the cotton trade picked up, then I went to work at Dunlop. John Connis were't carder. And with being out of the cotton for so long, it's a very funny thing, but when you go back in to be closed in, you get sleepy. And I worked on cards.

And John Connis's office were at bottom of my alley. It didn't matter, I could just stand up, but I'd fall asleep. I thought to myself one day, oh dear, I can't put up with this, because, I kept falling asleep. And John Connis was always shouting at me for doing it. So I thought I'd have to look for a fresh job.

*

So I went to the dole, and they was advertising jobs for the Naafi canteens. In these canteens they always had soldiers do it. But then they modernised them and made them into Naafi canteens. So, I applied for this business. They said, would you be a counter hand, or would you be in the beer bar, or would you be a trainee cook? So I said, well, I don't mind, I can do all three. So anyhow they said, well, be a trainee cook, so I said, alright. I went to Kent.

If you know Manston Aerodrome, it's outside Ramsgate and Margate, it's inbetween, in the field. We went there and the manageress must have thought that I was an experienced cook. Nobody's experienced when they've never seen such great big ovens as they had.

Have you ever come from public business to private business? It's a very funny thing. I'd come out of public business, then I went to the Naafi canteens you see. Now in a public, you encourage your customers. But you didn't need to encourage the army fellas, they were there anyhow.

One day, they was having the painters in, in Manston. And these painters were living on the site where we all were. I was on late duty, because the canteen used to open from ten till twelve at night-time, so the lads could have a drink or some supper before they went to bed, you see. Anyway, it wasn't that same night, it was another night when they was having a dance. These painters said to me, "Can we come to the dance?" I said, "Yes, course you can, anybody's allowed to come. It's on the site."

So, we went to the dance, and half way through the night when it was interval, these painters said, "By God, I am hungry." So I said, "Well, go to't canteen, and get a meal." They said, "We don't know whether we'd be allowed in or not." I said, "Oh, don't bother about that, you'll be allowed in with me." So we went to't canteen didn't we. Me, and four of the painters."

I ordered the supper for them. I thought I may as well have a cup of tea and sit down and be sociable. But the lady in charge saw me didn't she, through her office window. She said to the other girl that was on the canteen counter, "What the hell is Mary doing, in the men's canteen, with the painters?" This girl looked, she said, "She's having her supper." She said to me, "How dare you sit in the canteen, amongst all the men. You're not supposed to do." I said, "I were only bringing you some custom." She said, "What did you do before you's came here?" and I said, "Barmaid." She said, "Only a Lancashire lass, being a barmaid'd do such a thing."

Anyhow, from then she put me in the beer bar. We had them barrels of beer that you had to bend down to, to turn the tap. The manageress there said, didn't you come as cook, Mary?" I said, "Yes." She said, "Well, they want one in Dover. Would you go?" I said, "Yes, I'm not bothered." So I went to Dover.

The manageress there had a little poodle. Mind you, there were twenty-eight staff and you had to give them their breakfast. And she wanted her cup of tea in bed and her poodle's dinner. So I kicked the poodle over the other side of the kitchen. She didn't like it a bit. she said, "Have you fed my doggie?" I said, "No, I haven't fed your doggy," I said, "if you want your doggy feeding, feed it yourself. I have enough to feed without bothering about your doggie."

Then another night, she was taking doggie for a walk. She wanted everybody else to walk with her. I said, "You must be joking." I said, "I'm walking nowhere." So that, of course she didn't like. Because the others were docile and went walking with her. And I wouldn't do.

Another thing she did was, she told me to give them some sausages one morning, and I decided they weren't fresh. So I wouldn't cook them. I just told her, I said, "You're not on." She said why hadn't I given them to them? And why had I thrown them away? I said, "Because they are not fresh, and sausages that are not fresh are not fit for anybody." I said, "We don't want half the army poorly." So I threw them away, and she was mad. She 'phoned up the area manager and told him that I was unmanageable. I didn't bother, I just went to the't next one. They just move you, you see, they don't bother.

Then, there was a fella came in the canteen. He was one of the forcemen, and he did make me laugh. He had his moustache exactly like Players had on their packets of cigarettes. Tickled me to death. So I said to him when he came, "I'll have a Player."

*

We went back to Dover then. This was 1939 just before the war started. They brought all the regiments from India – the Black Watch, the King Shropshire Light Infantry, and the Southerners. There were three regiments in Dover. I used to like the Black Watch. They have lovely uniforms. And when they brought all these lads home, they also brought with them their wives and the children. We had to put palliasses all over the canteen floor for them to sleep on.

Anyhow, at that time, I was courting one of the young men there. And he said, "Do you know what you're going to do now when war starts?" I said, "I'll stop here." He said, "Don't stop here," he said, "Go home. Because, it'll be terrible in Dover when the war starts." He said, "Go home." Anyhow, I went home.

When I came up, I thought, What do you do now there's a war on? You don't know what to do, so I re-joined. They sent me to Shrewsbury. And the funny thing was, the King Shropshire Light Infantry was also transferred to Shewsbury. Which I didn't know until I went. We used to use a taxi man in Dover. Because we used to always ring the same one up, to take us back to barracks, rather than walk, because there's no buses in Dover. It's too steep. When I went in the canteen at first, who should be there but the taxi driver. He said, "Bloody hell, Mary," he said, "what are you doing here?" He said, "Having a change?" He said "I'll tell you what, that boyfriend of yours is here." I said, "Why are the King Shropshires here?" He said, "Yes." My husband were dispatch rider for the regiment.

This were the beginning of 1940. And the war had started in September 1939. So we decided then what to do, we said, "What shall we do?" So at finish, we decided we'd get married, rather than wait while after the war. So we did. We got married at the cathedral, Turnwalls, in Shrewsbury. The only person that were a catholic at my wedding were me. It wouldn't have been known before the war. We didn't even know the people that stood for us proper. So, that's when we got married, in 1940.

13 Vivienne Travis

I come from the paper shop, on Beursil Avenue. I come up every day with the papers, and generally have a chat with the patients. Also bring sweets up for the shop, anything that the shop needs. Tommy comes down occasionally with his order, and we bring it up.

My two children like coming up as well. Jennifer is two and a half, and she's been coming up since day one, it's like a second home. Patients, and staff particularly, know Jennifer better then they know us. She doesn't bother, she comes belting round, she plays with the toys in the toy box, to her it's just like home. She thinks it's great, coming to see the nurses. Certain people she got quite attached to, and she has chats to. She likes the budgie.

There was one particular old man that she liked. He always used to give her chocolate, and called her his little piece of fluff. She used to go to the drawer next to his bed every morning, and he used to give her a bar of chocolate. He was called Arthur. She couldn't really say 'Arthur' all that well, but we understood what she meant. She came one day and he'd unfortunately died that morning. We then had to try to explain to her, at eighteen months where he'd gone.

Occasionally sometimes now, she'll go to roughly where his bed was, and looks to see if Arthur's still there. He seems to have stuck in her mind. It comes and goes. If I ask her now, I imagine she'll say she knows nothing about Arthur. But if she comes up, she will go to a certain room, a certain bed, and have a look for him. She occasionally says, "Has Arthur gone to Jesus?"

I think it's a great place to come up to with children, it doesn't make them, hopefully, half as worried about whatever could happen to parents, or anybody when they die, not necessarily with cancer, but with anything else. It's a great place to come up to. There are days when we come up here when we're cheesed off with everything. By the time we've left here, we haven't the right to feel ..., and it does us the world of good.

14   Margaret Macdonald

Billy was a long distance lorry driver, continental. He used to go to various countries, such as Sweden, Germany, Greece, Turkey, Hungary, Czechoslovakia, Bulgaria, U.S.S.R.. He even went to Pakistan. And he used to go all over the continent, meet various people. He used to go to various places and he got to know a lot of people. Little boys and girls, he used to take them for runs in his truck and give them sweeties. They knew when he was coming, so they used to sit and wait, and wave. And he always used to go V with his fingers, Churchill. He's done that for ten years.

He could deliver anything from nylons, whisky, tractors, there was no set thing that he had to deliver. He used to take a load all the way back from various factories. He would go away for about three weeks sometimes, sometimes a fortnight, sometimes four, it just depended on where he was going. Some of the time he used to stop in lovely hotels. But he used to do a lot of his own cooking. He had all the facilities, it was a big sleeper car, a Scania.

I've been with him, to Romania and Baghdad and places. I went

Billy McDonald with his mate in the cab of his lorry.

with him on one trip and there was an accident. This particular lorry was carrying brandy. There was nobody hurt, fortunately. But there was an awful lot of tangles and we were there all day. And that was a bit embarassing because I needed to go to the toilet, and there were no toilet facilities, in the middle of nowhere. But we managed, then we gathered.

All the trucks used to gather. And whoever got at this hotel first put the kettle on. All the drivers would come round with their cups. I used to boil tea for them all and we'd have sandwiches. We used to have little parties. It was great really. There were other drivers' wives there. We would go out and have a meal, and have a few drinks, a few laughs and then carry on our merry little way the following morning, in different directions. Billy would say he was going to say Germany, well I'm going to Yugoslavia, but we'll meet at such and such a place, and they used to do that.

The continental drivers, marvellous community between them. If one was broke down and you saw him, that driver would stop until he either got sorted or taken to the next town so that he could 'phone in to his work. It was marvellous. You were never alone, there was always somebody going your way. You always arranged to meet at some point at the end of the night, or the end of two days, or, I'll be in Germany, Wednesday. Right, I'll see you there, we'll catch the ship back home. Surprising how they would meet up again.

He enjoyed it. It was a fascinating life for him. He really enjoyed it. He realised that as you get a little bit older, though he's not old, as you get a little bit older, he thought he would settle down and keep me company more. So he's still driving, heavy goods, but not abroad. He just used to go all over England and London and places like that, delivering suitcases. And he was quite content with that. And I had him home every week-end. I didn't mind him going away during the week, but he came home every week-end. He used to go away on Monday, and he would come home Tuesday, he would go away Wednesday, and he would come home Thursday, and then he was home for the rest of the week, which I really enjoyed.

15   Marie Gibbons

I'm a community Macmillan nurse, based in Rochdale, and we visit the hospice regularly, have meetings here once a week, also some of our patients are here. There are two types of Macmillan nurses, hospital based, and community based. I'm community based. I'm a State Registered Nurse and I've also got a community certificate, which is a district nurse certificate.

Our role is that we visit patients who are terminally ill in their home environment. We offer psychological support to the patient and their family, and we offer advice on pain and symptom control. The district nurses give physical care to the patient, and we complement them by giving our support in other ways.

Say a terminally ill man wants to stay at home to die, and his family want him to stay at home to die. If it was necessary, then the district nurses would go in and give physical care. The G.P. will obviously be involved. If there was any special problem, such as pain that's not easily controlled, or any other symptoms such as vomiting, nausea, constipation, then we're looked on as a resource to draw in other professionals. We would talk to the patients, and we'd give advice, and we'd see if there was any alternative, or any adjustment we could make to their treatment.

What's special about us is that we have time. We are given time to spend with patients, which is necessary to get a proper history. It could be that we spend all day with one particular patient. The district nurse has got a caseload, she's got other patients that need her, so her time is limited with every patient. We counsel patients, we talk to patients, we listen to patients, we offer support, and point families in the right direction if they need any other help.

We see the hospice really as of great benefit to us, because although the majority of our patients want to die at home, it's often necessary for the family to have a break, beacause of the burden of care. Or the patient himself may need pain and symptom control looking at by people who can be with him all the time over a twenty-four hour period. The hospice is a resource for us. We can refer our patients through to Dr Gartside and Matron. We welcome the philosophy of this hospice, that it's short stay.

We liase closely with the staff here, we've got a really good relationship. We meet once a week, every Tuesday morning with Matron, often Sister Beaumont, and Dr Gartside. We go through all the patients in the hospice, whether they're known to us, or whether they're likely to be needed to be known to us. We discuss any problems that we've got with patients outside. We may suggest that they come in for respite care, or for pain control.

That patients and family can have a break is of paramount importance to me. If patients can come in here for a short period, and be prepared to go back home again a little bit stronger, a little bit happier, and families are rested, then they can go on for much longer. If they've got problems outside, the hospice is somewhere they can come to be looked after.

As far as I'm concerned, it's just a pity that there's not more places like this. We're so lucky in Rochdale. I feel privileged as a Macmillan nurse to be able to tell the patients that they've got this facility.

Some patients at home, when they have got problems and we suggest the hospice, a lot of them are frightened of the word hospice, because they feel that it's a place where they end the rest of their days really. But sometimes it's difficult to get over to them that it's really not that at all, it's more like a nursing home, or it's a holiday for them. They can come in, have their symptoms relieved, then go back home again. Once they come in, they wonder why they were at all worried about it. Once they've seen what it's like, they feel so comfortable, and once they're discharged, they want to come back time and time again.

Matron's very good: if there is a patient who's apprehensive about coming in, then I have brought them up and shown them round, and had a cup of coffee here. Then they've gone home, made their mind up, and I've never heard of anybody yet saying no thank-you. It's always, well, can I come in yesterday?

16 Zeriah Moore

First impression, people were so very kind when I first came in. I came up last Friday, to actually see the place, and to find out whether I really like it. From the moment I entered the door, I don't think I could say no to come back, really. They were so welcoming, and so good with me and my visitors, it was fantastic. They really gave me that feeling that, you know, they have such caring ability. I was only here for a few hours, and they really put me at ease, I didn't feel apprehensive at all, afterwards.

I had a chat to Sister first, and then Matron came over, had a chat. My Macmillan nurse brought me. My daughter came round, and we were all welcome. Sister told me a little bit about the place, what they do and the rules that they've got, and regulations, visiting times and things like that. Then Matron came, she really welcomed me and she said, "Would you like to come back, if we offer you a place?" So I said straight away, I didn't mind, because I really didn't mind. The welcome was so great that you just couldn't refuse. So I said to her, "Yes, I would." She offered me a bed for Monday, it was a Friday. Before I'd realised I'd said yes, I'd already said yes.

Just went home and got a few things together, and my nurse brought us back on the Monday morning. My daughter came, and one of my friends. Once again, we were welcomed, like they've known us for a year. The surroundings are so beautiful, breathtaking.

I know I needed somewhere like this. At home, there's just me and my daughter. And it's been quite hard for my daughter over the past fifteen months I've been ill. It's just been her at home, doing things I've not been able to do, like shopping, washing, cooking, cleaning up. Some days I can see that it's so hard for her. She's been struggling along despite what. Before I became ill, she had some emotional problems of her own, which she had to cope with. Then this illness came along, which meant she was dealing with double problems really. And I think, for somebody like that, she has coped and is coping immaculately. She just turned twenty-one two weeks ago. It was her birthday on the fifteenth of January.

I got rather weepy, I'm afraid, as soon as I got in here. When I got in here, I started crying. But, it was, I think, over joy. So kind and helpful people are. That's all I've had since I've been here. Nobody's ever been unkind.

Everybody I've met has been so kind. They're either kind, and they come around, or they're still kind, and they stay away. I think some people are very frightened of the word cancer. I don't suppose I realied that until I became ill. I found myself, I didn't think anything about cancer, until I became ill. You hear so and so's got cancer. I'm a nurse myself, I've nursed terminally ill patients with cancer. But you don't know what it is till it happens to you, no matter what it is, it doesn't have to be cancer, it could be anything. You just don't know what it is until it happens to you.

But it's a shame that people are so frightened, because, it's not anything to be frightened of, it's just an illness. I might say, why me? Why not me? Cancer is not choosy. It can attack anyone, old, young, middle aged, the ill and the well. In fact it can attack anyone. Anyone's immune system that is so weak to allow it to enter their being. Those who are walking the street to-day can find they have cancer tomorrow.

So my advice really is to give a lot of your time and to try and be more open about it. Try and learn a bit more about it and then you'll be able to help people a lot more. Because by knowing about the disease, and knowing how it progresses, and how it can turn one's life upside-down, they give themselves a chance to be as helpful as they can. And if, God forbid, it happens to them, then they themselves will know what particular people have been through. That's my verdict on cancer. It's not a nice thing, it's not a nice thing at all. It takes over your body and just, well it's taken over my body and it's had real fun with it. I don't know how far it's going to go, but it's going to be getting worse every day.

There I was getting on with my life and wallop, bang, there it was in my left breast. I had a lumpectomy, but it returned. I had chemotherapy, yet again, it returned. I had a radical mastectomy. And, guess what? Yes, it returned. I had radiotherapy, but it returned even more aggressively. Only one more treatment left to try now – I was put on hormone therapy, together with steroids. Hormone therapy to help the cancer, steroids to help me get on with my life. It's a question mark whether it will work. A patient has to be patient.

I was just working like an ordinary person. Went to work every day, did my work, came back home. Just an ordinary mother. I brought up my daughter. I had two children. I didn't get much help, off the father. My eldest daughter, she's twenty-two, was sent to my parents when she was eleven months old. She was eleven months old and I was seven months pregnant with the little one. I've had contact as she's grown up through letters.

My father died in 1975, he died suddenly, he was only fifty-one. So, my daughter had to go and live with my sister. In fact she's younger than me, she just comes after me. My sister took my daughter, so she's lived with her since then. She's twenty-two.

*

I'm from Liberia on the west coast of Africa. There has been fighting since about 1989. The army took over the country in 1980, then the government took over the country, then finally the army took charge of the country. Obviously they weren't doing what they were supposed to do, so other leaders got a little bit fed up of it, and decided to retaliate. Fighting started.

There's no Liberia any more. It's completely destroyed. So many lives were lost. Many people fled the country to bordering countries. My sister, who actually has my daughter now, and her family, fled to Ghana. They're now living in the refugees' place, until perhaps things are sorted out a bit better. If the fighting stops completely, they can return back home.

But, like her, there's loads of people had to do the same thing. In fact they walked for four days in the bush, to get to their destination. No food, no water. Just the clothes they were wearing and just what they had on their feet. The youngest child was five. My sister has a daugher, she's the same age as my daughter, both twenty-two. She has an elder son, I think he's seventeen.

The day they were going, he was apparently doing a part-time job. They had to leave very urgently because the war just came into the area where they were living, they had to pick themselves up and more or less run off. And my little nephew wasn't home at the time. He didn't go with them. I think up until now, she doesn't know where he is. It's very very devastating. Last time she wrote to me she said she wanted to go back to Liberia to try and find him. So, I don't know whether she has done.

I believe the fighting has stopped a little bit. The people were trying to get some kind of interim government. Go in to try and

Zeriah's mother.

get the country on its feet again.

My mother, that's my mother's photograph behind me. I don't know, I cried for days, but, I haven't seen my Mum since my Dad died in 1975. It's been heartbreaking not even seeing her. For the war to take place and then for me to become ill. I missed her terribly. Cried loads of days for her. Before my sister left, my daughter said she saw my mother. She didn't want to leave, because, you know the older people, they get used to their surroundings, used to where they are, they don't want to come away. She said she didn't want to go to any strange country. She wanted to stay at home, despite what was going on around her. So she stayed. She's staying with one of my cousins I believe.

I've got a sister and a brother in America, quite a number of family in America. They ring me and give a bit of news. The last time I heard they said she was O.K., she was fairly well. But it breaks your heart to.... If I could just see her. Just hold her, you know? I admit it would make the world of difference to me. It's not been easy. But, a bit more tranquil the past week-end.

My brother used to work for the government of Liberia, the government that there was at the time that the war took place. He was Minister of Education. Like many countries, when fighting takes place, the government troops, or the rebel troops, try to get the other side. Or, if a lot of the government troops are killed, the government troops retaliate against their own people. And so my brother was unfortunately unmercifully killed like many other people in Liberia. But my sister said, I believe his hands were tied, and he was shot.

I couldn't believe it really. I only just come out of hospital after having radiotherapy, the day before. I cried the whole night. In fact the doctor had to come and put me under sedation. I just couldn't control myself, couldn't believe it. And a few days later, I heard through my sister in America that my uncle had been killed. Troops just went into his house and shot him. He was sitting in his armchair in the sitting room and they just burst into the house and shot him dead.

So, with all this news, it's not been easy really. I've tried to cope. You don't forget it but you just try to overcome it.

When there's a war takes place, so many people lose their lives. I suppose, in a way when you think of other people, you think that you're not alone, it's not just happened to you. So that in itself gives you a bit of encouragement to carry on. I think that's what's happened to me. I think of the poor little kids that have been orphaned, they have noone to look after them. My brother's wife, and his son, well I think up until now we don't know where they are. We don't know whether they're still in Liberia, or whether they were killed, don't know, just presumed missing. A lot of my family is presumed missing. Loads of other families have gone missing. But, that's how it is.

When the war has really come to an end, there's going to be a lot more people missing than we really know about. We won't really know who's missing and who's not missing, and who's dead and who's alive until the country is back on its feet again.

Liberia has been destroyed completely. I pray and hope, maybe not in my lifetime, that things will return, with God's help, to normal. Because it was a lovely country. Through greediness, and through power, it was so destroyed. I pray and hope that things, it will be hard for it to be the same again, but at least for it to be a country again. That's my wishes.

17 Marylyn and Kenneth Beaumont

Ken

I asked Mal. After she'd prompted me into it. Mal, or Mally, that's what I call her. Besides other things. We got married in the registry office, and we came up here for the blessing. It was a great suprise when we got up here that everybody was here. Flabbergasted. Very nice though.

I had a suit of my own actually. A friend of ours, my best man's wife, didn't want me to wear that, she wanted me to wear something else. So, she took me to Dennis Hope's and said I had to pick a suit. We were both arguing in the shop because I said something fit me and she said it didn't. It was like me and her being married, never mind me and Mal.

Very hectic day. To start off, we went to the registry office and got married, early in the morning. And then we went for a champagne breakfast that my best man and his wife laid on. Then we went home, put us feet up for five minutes, and came up here. Only expected to be here about ten minutes, quarter of an hour. Must have been here a couple of hours.

I remember Dr Bob saying congratulations, and me turning round and saying congratualations to him. Forgetting it was my wedding, I thought it was his.

The day went smashing. Everything just fell into place, considering we only had three days to prepare it. So if anybody's getting married, do it in three days. Don't panic, get married and have done with it. Next time I get married, I'll know, I'll do it in two days.

It was a very nice experience. I shouldn't think it'll be one that me and Mal would ever forget. We enjoyed ourselves immensely. We've still got the big champagne bottle that was opened up for us on that day.

Marylyn

Bearing in mind the cost of getting engaged, we decided just to skip that and get married. We decided we'd go down to the registry office to register. We asked when he could fit it in. Ken said, "Can you do it tomorrow?" And the man said, "No, you need twenty-four hours' notice." I was thinking six weeks in advance, and he said, "I can fit you in on Saturday morning at nine o'clock," and we said yes. So, the legalities of it were sorted out, except we needed a special license. We came away.

I came into work, Thursday, told Matron. She suggested did we

Ken and Marylyn on their wedding day.

want to come up afterwards to the Hospice. One thing led to another. There was a blessing arranged in the chapel. It meant we could share it, with the people that I felt — Ken wasn't working here then — were like an extended family.

Ian, the Minister came up, that Thursday afternoon. I asked him, "How are you fixed for Saturday?" So we went off and produced a marriage ceremony, and had it photocopied. Somebody fixed up an organist, I don't know who, but the organist was playing, which was lovely. Dr Gartside videoed the wedding. We had champagne, and they made a wedding cake in two days.

My friend said to me, "What are you going to wear?" I was going to wear a navy blue suit and a white blouse. I could tell by the expression on her face that that wasn't really acceptable. She dragged Ken off to Dennis Hope's to hire a suit. This is Thursday afternoon, and Friday, I went to a wedding dress hire shop. She said, "I'll have it ready for tomorrow?" I stood there while she altered it, and took it home. I got my dress, my tights, my shoes, and head-dress and everything from there. All wrapped up in a nice little package.

When we came up for the day, I can truthfully say, with my hand on my heart, it's one of the nicest days I've had. Everybody put so much into it, and a lot of people came in their own time. It was lovely. It was as if months and months of planning had gone into it. So, now I'm setting up budget weddings.

18   Sidney Thomason

Fantastic. I didn't think that anything like this existed. Been in hospitals, plenty of hospitals, but, nothing like this, are they? I think they're marvellous, the nurses, they couldn't do any more for you. The reason being maybe, that they enjoy their work. They seem a happy crowd here. I've enjoyed my stay. Wonderful place. You don't need to go to heaven to meet the angels.

I was a colour mixer for book cloth. Good books, I mean, you don't get many to-day, but good books have always got a backing on them. Different colours. If you get, say the A.A. Handbook, there's always a kind of a cloth back on them. I used to do the colours for that kind of thing. They were very fussy, the bookbinders. You might send them a thousands yards of a colour that they ask for. And then maybe the next seven yards have gone too slightly off colour. They wouldn't have it. And yet the customer would never see it.

I started working life as a baker and confectioner. And then went in the Army. Six years in the Army. For the biggest part of that, I was a hospital cook. Being a baker and confectioner, when they asked for volunteers, I volunteered, of course. And we had the best training anyone could have with all the high chefs. From the Waldorf and all that. Trained by them. The Army never did things by half, did they? Always did something good. So that was my life until I was about thirty. I went into the army as a single man, and came out with a wife and two kids.

Got married didn't I. And never regretted it. Forty-six years we've been married. And we've never had one argument.

I'd like to say thank-you for every minute we've had together. It's been paradise. Especially for these last months. She's had so much to do. Selling the house, and getting a flat. She must be feeling worn out. And I thank her for doing that.

19   Margaret Geoghegan

Both my parents and my husband died of cancer. I'd had a Red Cross nursing background, and so was able to look after my husband till he died, at home.

I worked, as a ward clerk, on a male medical ward. One day I was sitting in the ward office at Birch Hill Hospital, and the sister-in-charge and I were talking about a hospice and I said, "Do you really think that people would support us?" What she did was, she just leaned down and got her handbag up, she put a five pound note on the table, and she said, "Well there you are Margaret, there's your first donation. If you don't go now, you're getting money under false pretences."

That was the spurt we needed. So, we decided that we'd launch in Rochdale, on the 8th May 1983, on the Tuesday, in Middleton on the 10th on the Thursday, and in Heywood on the following Tuesday. We didn't really know what we were going to do on this first Tuesday in Rochdale. Nobody else wanted to speak. I'd collected quite a lot of information from hospices, so we decided that we'd have a screen with all this information put on.

We decided we wanted a colour. Well, being election year, there was so much red, blue and yellow about, we decided that we'd go for green. We said, if we're going to launch, then we needed some kind of a badge. I like the Heart Foundation badge, the little red square, rather than a round button type of thing, which I thought wasn't very elegant. I found out where they got their badges from, and I rang this man in London. He wanted to know what colour, and I said, a nice grass green. He said, "I've got forty-eight shades of green, you'll have to send me a sample."

Betty Portman and I went round her house, and we looked at everything, curtain linings, seat covers, cushion covers, blankets, you name it, went through the embroidery box, looking for the shade of green. And we kept saying, "No, that's not it, that's not it. No, I don't like that." Then, suddenly, there was a Marks and Spencer's bag on a chair. I said, "That's what we want." So we cut the corner off the end of a Marks and Spencer's bag.

The time came for the first launch on the Tuesday. We'd pinned all the information we had on this screen. Betty had done this big flower arrangement to go on the table. We went to St. Chad's Hall, near the Parish Church and as we arrived, the caretaker said. "I've put all the chairs out." I said, "What have you done that for?" He said, "Well, we thought we'd put them all out, just in case." So I said, "Well, people will just have to come and sit at the front that's all, if there are only a few in."

We were all so busy, and suddenly, somebody came in and said, "Have you looked in the hall, Margaret?" I said, "No, I don't want to." I was quite nervous enough about having to say my piece as it was." Then suddenly, the mayor's attendant came over, Barry. He often reminds me of it, he said, "Mrs Geoghegan, will you come and receive the Mayor, and Mayoress." Well, I knew the Mayor and Mayoress very well, they were friends. I went across, and the Mayor said, "Isn't it great Margaret, look at all these people. It's going to be a great night this, great." I said, "That's not how I feel." I was shaking like a leaf.

Eventually the hall was absolutely cram jammed full, and people were standing at the back, which frightened me to death. Obviously I'd made some notes, and I said we'd done research and we'd looked at numbers and viability. We had a very good meeting, everybody was in agreement, and we decided to go ahead and launch the appeal. We had a cheque presented by Roch Valley School, that was a nice surprise. But the funny thing was, we never thought about having a collection. Never entered our heads. But as people were going out, they were walking past the table where all the seven trustees were sitting, and people were dropping pound notes and five pound notes on the table.

On the Tuesday we were going to Heywood. It was great that night. There were about two hundred people. We got the first real public response in Heywood. Two people stood up.

One was a young man, and he said that for the past eight months, he'd been taking his mother-in-law every day to the hospice in Cheadle. And if I remember rightly, it was a round journey of something like forty miles. He's been taking his mother-in-law to visit her husband every night. He said it was ruining their lives, it was ruining their family life, and his mother-in-law's life, dragging her down, and we needed a hospice of our own nearer.

Then there was another girl, her father had died over Christmas. Her and her mother did say they would try and look after him at home, but apparently it became evident that he was in such a distressing state, that they got to the stage where they just couldn't cope. She said that they'd rung hospices, Elland, they even rang the hospice in Sheffield, to try and get him in. Just to relieve the pressure a bit for a few days. Again, she said that they need a hospice nearer. This girl actually started the first support group that we had, which was in Heywood, at that meeting. I think about half a dozen people joined. So that was great.

I remember going to speak at a school. We had to be there for half past eight in the morning. When we got in the hall, it was a wooden floor, and can you imagine what my heels were like, going clack, clack, clack, across this wooden floor. It was an assembly at the upper school with about four hundred children.

What I didn't know at the time was that one of the pupil's parent's had just died with cancer. Plus that fact that the deputy head had already had a cancer operation. This school used to give half the money that was raised at the Christmas Fair to the mayor's charity every year, the other half was given to a charity of the pupil's choice.

I was saying that we would need special beds, not only for the benefit of the patients, but also for the benefit of nurses. This boy asked me from the hall, how much these beds would cost. I had coffee afterwards with the headmaster in his room, and his secretary came and said, there are two young men here who want to have a word with you. They were two of the pupils, the head boy, and another pupil. They said, "You know that bed you want, well, we're going to buy you one." They did, they raised the money the following year.

One Spring Day, we decided that we'd dig the first sods. We put an advert in the paper, if anyone was interested, anyone who'd helped us in any way, if they would like to come along and help us dig the sods, they would be welcome.

We had a formal digging first of all, then it was everybody. But I only wish we had had it on video. If you'd have seen the people coming up the hill, with spades over their shoulders – I put in the advert, please bring your own spade – and children with little spades, honestly, we still talk about it, people still talk about it. We had a great day. There was a troupe of local morris dancers who met at the pub at the bottom of the road, and when they heard about it, they all came in costume, to provide some entertainment. It was just the right touch.

There were only three of us for a long time doing things. I'm afraid they were coerced into doing all kinds of things they'd never done in their lives before.

We went into this airfield to see this parachute jump. It was the most torrential rain I'd ever known. We had to drive through this airfield, and we kept going through gates. I made Betty Portman get out to keep opening the gates. Betty got out once and slammed the door and the window dropped. I had a piece of string in the car and we had to tie the window up. We got to the airfield and it had rained solidly from the night before. After we'd been there a couple of hours it was obvious that there weren't going to be any drops that day, so, we came away.

On our way back, we got to Grange-over-Sands, and I said, "Well,

I don't care, I'm going to have a cup of tea." We walked into this cafe, I sat down, and water ran down our legs, and I said, "Do you know, my knickers are wet." And everybody else said, "Yes, so are mine." I don't think I've ever been drenched to my skin before, but we really were that day, we were sopping wet through. And all these people were just sitting up there and waiting to jump out of a plane. We just sat there and laughed.

20   Violet Davies

They call me Vi.

Oh marvellous. Oh I do really, yes. I wish I'd come here when Beryl (Macmillan Nurse) asked me in the beginning. I come in yesterday. I couldn't lift that leg, I were in that much pain. And the drugs I'm having now are making me walk a lot better, without the continuous pain. It was hopeless. If I'd've had trousers on I couldn't pull them up with that hand. I could have screamed the roof off. Just shows what it does overnight. Oh, they're wonderful.

I don't think they should have to be run by charity. They could go private, and then where would we all be? They should be paid without charity, having to collect off other people. I mean by all means let's all give something, I don't mind to that. Even if it were kept by the state, we'd still give. They come round for charity and you give more than you do for others. Government should pay, on its own.

I'm glad there's one, I am.

*

I worked all my life, since I were fourteen. I was a weaver. I left school on a Friday. I left at Easter. It'd be before Good Friday. You didn't have big holidays like you have now. You only got a week's holiday. Mill only closed for one week. Anyway, after Easter, went back to learn to weave with my mother. Well, I cried. I come home, I says, "I don't like weaving. I won't make a weaver." "You'll make a weaver by time I've done with you." I thought, "Yes, I bet I will an' all." And I says to our Nan, "No getting out of this." "No," she says, "I know you're not, I won't neither."

We were all in't same mill, Peel Mill, Accrington. She went winding, and my mother were weaving, and our Nellie's husband were a spinning master. So you couldn't..., some would say, "Oh, I'm not going in to-day, I'm off," because they were being taught by someone else. Not like with my mother. "They're not going in. Well you are, whether they are or not." She made me learn. I'd got two looms, I hadn't been there long. I ended up with six looms. Material for the Airforce, for the Army, the Navy. Then I went velvet weaving.

The war broke out, and we all went to work in Woolwich Arsenal at London. Ammunitions. You go underneath the ground by train. We was bombed out. Just because they were underground, doesn't say they couldn't get you. They could. We were making tanks actually. It was very hot. When the hooter went you had to go and take cover.

I came home, we were on nights. It was about seven o'clock. I had a verandah on the house down there. I was stood on the landing. And this German plane came right up, he were low, and I could see his face in it. If I hadn't have gone right down he'd have shot me, because he was so near. He dived so low we could see his face.

We used to have a great big, we called her Bertha, it was a big gun. And she used to come right in the main roads, where the buses would run during the day. It used to go, "Bum, bum, bum." We used to say, "Oh, there's Old Bertha going."

But, we never lost hope. We knew that we'd beat them in the end. We never let go. It's like they say, there'll always be an England, there always will.

We used to go out, you know, and I'm going up the street with my friend, and I says, Yankie boy over there's nodding at you, don't bring me into it." She said, "I won't be a minute." Her husband were away in't Army. I saw them giving her this big parcel, shoving it in her bag. No wonder she'd a big shopping bag with her. I said, "We're not going shopping to-day. We'll get nothing anyway with big bag like that, we're rationed."

We went in, we always used to go to each other's, we went in to have a cup of coffee, and she opens her bag. It were a great big ham. "Good Lord, where've you got that? It'll feed a thousand that. What you going to do with it, I hope you're going to give somebody else some." She said "Yes, I'm going to give you some." "No, don't give me none, because, my husband'll play pop. He'd think I were knocking about wi' 'em. No, he's due home at week-end." "Alright," she says, "I'll do it myself." "Well, you'd better," I says, "because it'll only go off."

People were glad of it. They were bringing cheese in. And the kids, "Any chocolate?" They like the foreign chocolate. They could get cigarettes where our lads couldn't. It was done really underneath a lot of it. Cheese, we were queueing up. And anyone that knew it, if they found out, they'd go to the army barracks and tell, if they weren't getting any. They'd go and split on them.

I've been in friends' that I know haven't had as many coupons as we had, but still had plenty. And he used to say to me, "Why do you go?" "I don't get no stuff off her, she's my friend and I'm not falling out with her. What they do is their business, not mine."

And you know how they talk, "there'll be kiddies running all over the place," and they were right. I says, "Well that's their look out, not mine. So long as I don't do it, I'm all right." There were some nice lads in't airforce, there were a lot of nice yanks, but there were these that... you know, well, as we said, that's their business, not ours.

I wish there'd been some of these places for the lads when they come out. To be looked after and paid for, like they are here.

And you never see a long face coming. Where when you worked in the mill, you used to say, "Oh no, not again." You don't see that expression on their faces here. They've got that lovely look that cheers you up, and you think, well, at least I've got another day. Because we know what's going to happen. They build you up. They give you that will to keep going on for as long as you can.

21   Dorothy Taylor

As a volunteer nurse, I am, I feel, a back-up for the staff nurses that are working here, doing everything for the care of the patients while they are in the hospice.

I trained as an S.R.N. as a mature student, and I have been in the Red Cross Society. I had worked in a hospital, as a volunteer under the old voluntary aid detachment. Then when I did my general training I realized that terminal care needed more specialised nursing than I felt was available at the time. I supported the start of the hospice movement in Rochdale with being in the Red Cross, and also as a trained nurse who has seen general care in hospital.

I come in, in a morning, and I then am given a report of the patient. It's a report of how they have been, where they are in their care, and what is necessary in that day for their care.

It's high dependency care, because a lot of them are unable to do the basic care they need for themselves, and generally to listen to them. I think the basic thing you can do is to help the patient help themselves. Being independent as long as they can is a morale booster. It's not taking over the functions of the patient, it is supporting and extending what the patient can do, by knowing the stage of their illness and when intervention is necessary and helpful.

I come one day a week, but funnily enough I have been called in to do extra duties. The only way they know I'm a volunteer is it's actually on my badge. There's no role difference and I don't think the patients see any difference either, I hope they don't. Even though it's voluntary, I feel that because of my expertise, I can give a lot to the hospice.

I've been very very impressed by the care of the carers, and the staff. I feel it is what I envisaged when the hospice was mentioned for Rochdale.

22 Lilian Owinor

I worked in a mill, winding cotton. They're no longer up, these properties now. There were quite many in Oldham, where I lived. So you could go out of one place and choose another. It was hard work. You'd have to be up soon. They started about half seven. They worked Saturday mornings in them days. They don't do Saturdays now. Everything's altered in that line of business. You worked then till half fiveish, going home in the dark, snowing, whatever it was doing. It was too noisy to talk in the mill. You got used to talking to one another by having signs. But you were most interested in time to go home. I never liked it. They certainly made you work hard for what pay you got.

I eventually left. Well, my health wasn't good. I just stayed at home. That's all there is really. I can't turn round and say, I really enjoyed doing that job. I didn't, I didn't like it.

I suppose most women want a nice home and family really. I suppose I enjoyed better being at home, because that's all I was fit for. I've had to be trying to fight my health for most of my life. And it's been jolly hard work. I've been ailing on and off since I was about thirty. I have to watch how much I rest. So I've never really gone out a lot. I've made quite nice friends along the road.

I went to Christie's. And I went to the nursing home, but I only stayed three days there. It wasn't suitable. My daughter and son-in-law, there's a place near them, not too far away. It's just been built. They think I'd be better going there. Obviously can't stay here. So next week, I'd like to see the place. Rather than just accept it without seeing it.

It's very good here, marvellous how they do things. They've controlled my pain. That's what I wanted. If I can get the use back in my legs, I feel I've beaten the situation. But they're trembling, and I can't seem to control that, unless it's the tablets that do it. I'd be sort of more content, because, if you think you've achieved something... You think that you're getting the best help that you can. But this lot's beat me. I've never been like this before, not as bad as this. This came on suddenly in both my legs. I've never experienced that before. I was a good walker before. I used to love going walks, being out in the fresh air. I've been fortunate in having a garden in most places I've lived. But of course I can't do gardening now. I feel that I've come to a part of my life where I'll be more handicapped than I ever was.

But my joy in life is having Susan and her little boy and little baby. I really enjoy that part. The little girl's four months old. The little boy's four. I feel that having them is giving me the courage to carry on with this.

I shall probably look back on this experience later on in life, and think it was lovely. It's not like in hospital here. It can be noisy at night in hospitals.

23 Dr Gartside

For thirty-two years I was a G.P., a senior partner in probably the largest practice in town, which I enjoyed very much. I felt it was really my vocation in life. But when my wife died, it was very difficult to be a G.P.. For instance, when you're on call and called out, there's no one at home to answer the 'phone. I bought an answering machine. But then I began to think that perhaps some really old grandma who it was difficult enough to get a story off anyway when you were talking to them, would find it difficult to leave a message on a machine. They can't understand why the machine won't talk back to them. And my life seemed to get so busy, there just weren't enough hours in the day, really.

I was approached one day, and asked if I would be interested in

Notice board showing staff members.

becoming medical director of the hospice, which was about to open within the next few months. So I gave the matter a lot of thought, looked at it from all different aspects. I met with the committee, they felt that they could offer me the post. So after many sleepless nights, I finally said yes, I would change my vocation in medicine.

I came into post on the first of July 1989. We were expecting at that stage that the hospice would open then. In fact, it didn't, because of various legal complications, it wasn't possible to open until October. It was the ninth of October 1989 when we actually opened. And we opened with two patients only that day, on a planned basis. And we worked very hard trying to just two patients, get them set up into a brand new regime. We'd had three months preparing how we were going to do things, what we would need to run it, engaging staff, trying to train the staff and so on.

It was all a very fascinating phase in life. A complete about turn for me. To plough through vast numbers of patients, like a sausage factory, seeing fresh patients every five minutes, doing a lot of visits in their homes, being on call, chairing the practice meetings. I was also a member of the Family Practitioner Committee as it was then, chairman of some of its sub-committees, I was the G.P. member of the health authority and I was the chairman of the local medical committee as well. I really had a very busy life indeed.

My earnings dropped dramatically, but I think I've been a lot happier. I was very exhausted I think at times, trying to run the house, a big garden, and two dogs to look after. I had to learn all about how to cope with living on my own, cleaning, washing, ironing, shopping, it was all strange really. And there just weren't enough hours in the day, I'm afraid.

So this life is at a more settled pace. The stresses are undoubtedly not as severe as they were. I now feel I can practise medicine in a much more sensibly paced life. I feel that I've got time to spend with the patients, and I just don't deal with as many. But all the patients here genuinely need a lot of help. We get nobody here with nothing wrong with them. Patients in General Practice wouldn't come to you and say "There's nothing wrong with me," not very often. They would occasionally. Perhaps fit people would come and say there was something they wanted your opinion about, or there might be a healthy child for assessment. Or I might be seeing a lady for a smear, there'd be nothing wrong with her. But the vast majority of people would believe there was a possibility at any rate that there was something wrong with them. Anxiety played a large part in symptomatology. And then many people were chronically ill and needed routine checking and prescribing for. Quite a lot just needed their hands holding and someone to talk to. It was very difficult to accommodate everybody's requirements in the limited amount of time and space that you had got.

The first thing that the patients here need, I think, is some understanding. They often need time. They need to be able to talk, to relate to the staff that they're being cared for by. They do not want to be patronised. Some don't want to talk at all about what's wrong with them. Some are very keen to be able to talk about what's wrong with them, and have someone who's willing to listen, without the emotional barriers that you get amongst your own family.

In drug therapy that we use here, nearly all the drugs are potent. We use a lot of opiates, morphine qnd diamorphine in particular. These, I think, are very very valuable in the caring for patients with terminal cancer, which is ninety-five percent of our work here. Pain relief is very important, and relief of nausea and vomiting. Problems with constipation are frequent with our patients, partly because of the drugs that they're having to take which do constipate people. And also immobility and lack of the ability to eat well. So that's another thing, maintaining nutrition; trying to avoid pressure sores, trying to support them physically and emotionally, trying to care for the relatives and support them as well. These are the main features of the care that the patients need here.

In addition, we see people in Daycare. I try to offer my services if anybody wants to see me and to talk with me each time they come.

I also consult with other doctors and advise them on problems that they may be meeting in caring for their patients, but perhaps at that stage that patient doesn't wish to come into the hospice.

And, I suppose it's a relatively small part of my job, but I do sometimes have to go around and give talks, lectures and so on. Which I'm not quite keen on. I'm not gifted in that particular field. I've spent my life on a one to one basis, and to address an audience doesn't come too easily. I think it's a bit less traumatic now than it used to be.

I feel that there's only one certain thing in life, and that's that one day your life will end. I believe that we should all keep that at the back of our minds, and that you should try to pack as much into life as possible and make every day count. We should try and help our fellow human beings along the way, because by doing so, we undoubtedly gain one of the most uplifting things that human beings can gain really. I think to put it in a nutshell, that's got a lot to do with it.

If, when a life has to finish, it can finish in a dignified, stress-free and comfortable way, then I feel that that's been a very useful thing. I do not feel that we've been no use just because a patient dies.

24   Vanessa Tonks

Benji looks like a walking rug on four legs. He's four and a half. He's a cross between a Chow and a Labrador. We got him from the R.S.P.C.A. three years ago. He eats anything, chocolates, sweets, biscuits, toast, absolutely anything, cream crackers. He doesn't eat stuff like beans, anything like that.

He's soft. He always wants attention. He's got a nice face. He goes after 't budgie.

I like taking him out. For a walk along the canal.

*

My room is small. It's got a telly in it, and a 'phone. It's really small, with pale blue wallpaper with flowers on it. Two chests of drawers and a bookshelf. That's all you can get in it. I have a typewriter as well, but not in my bedroom, there's nowhere for it to go. I used to do typing at school. I did do office work for a while, then I changed to sewing. I didn't like the supervisor though, that's why I changed. But I enjoyed it though.

When I'm like this, I'd rather be downstairs, than upstairs, on my own. I might be going home soon. I might be able to go home if we can cope.

25 George Kearton

I view my role as being to encourage people to give money and other support to the hospice. By encourage, I mean make them aware of what the hospice is, and giving them the opportunity to support the hospice by creating ways that they can help us, either financially or with gifts in kind, or with their physical help at fundraising and other hospice events.

If you want a picture of it, and this is true for any voluntary organization, imagine a river of goodwill, of pound notes, pound coins, donations, flowing through the community. On either side of that river there are lots of fields, which are the charities concerned. They need that water from that river, they need that money. The only charities that are going to successfully get that support, are those who have a channel from their own activities out to the community river of money. We have to make it easy for people to give money, so that they give it to us, rather than some other charity.

For example, you've got collecting boxes, you make sure that you've got them in shops that people go into. If you've got a membership scheme, you make sure that membership forms are available, and you make sure that everybody knows that you've got a membership scheme. If you're doing a promotion or an event like, for example, house to house collections, you give people the opportunity to come back to you and say, "Here we are, we want to help you."

It's not a matter of necessarily thinking of events, it's looking at things that we're already doing to fundraise, and make sure that they're done as well as they possibly can be done. And making sure that everyone in the district has got that opportunity to support the hospice. It's an educational role as well as a purely fundraising one, because if people don't know what the hospice is about, they won't necessarily want to help us.

26   Ivy Ashton

The thought of the hospice at one time would have filled me with dread. I was rushed into here because I was so ill. And I couldn't have believed that any place could have done me so much good. From the point of view of the peace and the calm and the caring. A lot of people read, and do other things, and I am quite content to sit here, or lie here, and just let the calm and the peace flow. To me that is the best therapy, to see all these wonderful people, caring. And all the volunteer people, doing it all for love, is an eye-opener. The hospice has done me a world of good, from a spiritual point of view.

27   Ian Thompson

I aim to come into the hospice at least once a week, which, generally speaking is on a Friday afternoon. Regardless of how many patients are in, I try and spend the whole afternoon here.

Primarily I come to talk first to all of the patients. They come in with varying degrees of Christian faith, but I don't see my role as being related just to those who express faith in God. I see myself as somebody whom perhaps they'll talk to, whereas they may not talk to other people. It doesn't always work that way. Sometimes I feel I can be almost a target. Once or twice I've come in, and patients have been very angry. Seeing me, representing in their mind, God, they then shout at me. If they do that, it might spare a member of the family who may get it. That anger, if it's there has to come out. So I try and latch on to any particular problems and difficulties.

Some patients, because I am who I am, I can sense that they're drawing back, because maybe they feel I'm going to preach at them, or they've had bad experiences of clergy in the past. So, people's responses vary according to preconceived ideas, I suppose.

But then, I also try to spend time, talking to the staff, and listening to what they've got to say. Again, it's difficult because they're very busy. One thing that I think the hospice is trying to do is be supportive to one another. But there's still that feeling, I think, that if you admit that you're finding something a problem, then you're admitting defeat, you're admitting that you can't cope as well as other people. So it's not always easy to dig below the surface and find out what's really going on in people's minds.

Also, coming on a Friday afternoon is quite useful, because very often the patients have visitors, so as well as talking to the patients, it's quite illuminating to talk to relatives as well. They come in with all sorts of different feelings. Some of them are relieved because obviously they've got a two week break and they can regain their strength. Some of them come in feeling very guilty that their relative has been shoved into the hospice and they see that as a failure. Some just are totally confused by the whole experience, they're not quite sure what's going on. And they need as much support as the patient themselves.

Linked with that, I do provide I suppose what you'd call a normal church service for people that want communion. But I see that very much as a secondary thing. I also organize the rota for Sunday afternoon services, so that there's a variety of churches coming in. Again, I try to ensure that the Sunday afternoon service is very informal, something that people will be able to go to who've got no church background at all. So that tends not to be a communion service, or a sacramental service, it's something for everybody, hopefully.

I try and find out, first of all, how a patient is reacting to their illness. I think sometimes people are frightened of talking to me because they might, underneath, feel very angry, and the last thing they want to hear about is a God who loves them. They're feeling angry, they're feeling resentful, they can't accept that God cares, otherwise he wouldn't have allowed this thing to happen. So what I try to do is to let them see that it's O.K. to shout at God, to let off steam, and to reassure them that whatever they say, whatever they feel, even if they can't accept God in the way that I do, he still cares for them, and wants to assure them of his love and his protection and give them his peace.

I used to say all that in a hollow way, because I'd never experienced any kind of bereavement or sadness in my own life. I'm sure, if people could have spoken to me a few years ago, they'd have perhaps recognized that what I was saying was something I'd learnt rather than something I knew.

It was only as a result of my father's own terminal illness that I discovered that it worked in practice. I went through all the feelings of anger and resentment, but through it all I still felt very surrounded by God, and what he wanted for me. It was a real joy, despite Dad's illness, to be able to talk to him about God. He was a man, who again, had never really given God much thought. I think he accepted that there was something greater than ourselves, but he wouldn't know how to articulate that. Being ill gave the opportunity to talk to him about God, which is something I felt nervous about in the beginning. I didn't want him to feel that I was shoving it down his throat, but it was something that came from him.

He asked me to do things for him, to tell him things. He even wanted me to take him to chuch to pray, a thing that I'd never been able to do with Dad before. And so now, I feel at least, even if people cannot accept what I'm saying, I do know, that it's real rather than something that's been learned from a book. It's worked out in my own experience, and I try to share that experience with others.

28   Ernest Prestwood

It's the anniversary of my wife's death in the hospice. I had a word with the doctor and the matron a few weeks ago and asked if it would be right for me to come in to-day and they said yes. I've had lunch and met all the nurses. It's been very pleasant. I see one nurse and she'll tell the others I'm here. They come and find me. I don't have to go and look for them.

When Amelia came here she came in the doors, and walking into this place was the best thing that ever happened to her. I've never regretted her coming in here. I don't think she could have been better looked after anywhere by anybody.

29   Kay Scott

It stems back from my mother, who was taken into hospital when I was eighteen years of age and she was thirty-seven. She walked into hospital on the Tuesday and died on the Sunday, having a lot of pain, and very little understanding from the people round her. I found that extremely distressing.

There's been a number of things that have happened in my lifetime that made me realize that I was unable to cope with terminal illness. Losing my first child. Having a girl that started training with me that had the same cancer as my husband, which is Hodgkin's. And watching my husband go through the stages of saying, "Why me?" "How long will it be?" "Will you give me something if I'm suffering?" "You won't let me suffer?"

The inadequacy of him going to Christie's, and that was many years ago, I'm going back twenty years. He got a lot of support, but I got very little. I was told to go to the doctor and get some tranquillizers when I asked for the results of the test on how far the disease had progressed.

With the friend, whereas my husband got better, she deteriorated. In fact I nursed her on the ward when she died. It was so noisy, and we felt inadequate. You couldn't talk to them as a family, and once she had died, the family had to go away. We had to battle with doctors, trying to get them to give correct medication to give the symptom relief that the patients needed. It was a great strain. And you can understand it from their point of view because in hospital, it's their philosophy to get people better. They're worried about the ethics of giving too high a dosage. Therefore the patients have a lot of pain and distressing symptoms.

So that when the hospice was talked about in Rochdale, I was very interested in the job of matron. Even with the worries of whether there could be enough money, whether it would be viable and whether it would take off. I thought it would be nice to finish my career, with ten years left, in a field that I've always felt that there've been some inadequacies.

I felt with the experiences I'd had, we could perhaps get it right within the hospice. And that's why I applied for the job.

When a patient comes into the hospice, they come with their family. You're treating a group of people. The biggest fear when they come into the hospice is that they are never going to go out again. There's a lot of guilt within the family because they haven't coped at home.

We try to involve the family. If you can reassure the family that you're going to treat the patient the same way as they did at home, they will be much happier. They know, firstly that you've listened to them, and that they're leaving them somewhere where the worries that they have have been taken into consideration.

It's vital when somebody comes in that there's time to be able to absorb all this information. It's important that you leave them when they come, to absorb the surroundings, and to be able to settle in and put their things away before you start firing questions. So that they have a drink, and they put their things away. Then I take their nurse and doctor round and introduce them. Usually that nurse ends up being their favourite nurse. She's the one they can unburden all their problems to, about their illness, from the beginning.

The way we admit patients is totally different to a hospital because it's not yes and no questions. They're open-ended questions. And you're getting the patient, and the family separately, talking about what they know, how much they know, what their expectations are, and what we're going to do for them. I believe that they should participate in their own care, they should understand what we're doing and why we're doing it. If they're not happy, we shouldn't be doing it.

I also think that as the disease progresses, whether they're getting better or getting worse, it's collectively talked about. So that you bring the family together, if you can. They've all got emotions that need help.

If somebody dies, the way they leave the building is as important as the way they came in. The family are given time at the bedside to spend as long as they wish. A sitting room is available for the family to spend some time together. The patient stays on their own bed, and in their own clothes. Death is very open in a hospice, there's no closing curtains round. Very often the relatives, because they've been visiting various patients, have got very close, and it's a comfort to them to see what's happening. The patient is brought over to the Rose Room, and the family are escorted in. They can spend as much time as they like here with them. And if they wish to come back in the middle of the night, or the following day, then that's what they should be able to do.

I had a very horrific ... when my mother died. I wasn't actually there when she died, because I'd been on duty. I went up to the ward and they sent me up to the mortuary. And they actually pulled her out of a fridge. And I will never forget that, to my dying day. Now I can still weep about it. I have never got over that.

It's been extremely difficult trying to get across what a hospice is about. Many people think it's just for somebody to come and die here. But that wouldn't be giving enough to people who are tired, many months before. If they know that there's a lifeline here, where a patient can come in for a couple of weeks, they can cope better. Holiday relief for patients enables the carers to have a holiday too. And it's a comfort to know this service is available at a later date.

We're still trying to get the message across, that it's not only for people who are at the terminal stage of dying. Although we don't do active treatment, we certainly encourage people to come, to make their life a much better quality, with a goal every day. So that they can go home, and life becomes more normal. We encourage patients to get dressed and go to the dining room. It's much better as a family to be able to cope with that, than lying in a bed worrying about the illness or when you're going to die.

By doing creative activities, something can be left for relatives and friends. It's so comforting for the family to know that these things are happening while they're not with them. Whether it's painting, writing, craftwork, or a trip to the pub, they've achieved something.

People should contact their G.P., or the Macmillan nurse, or the hospice for advice. Because of the short-term care policy here, a bed can be offered, normally, within twenty-four hours.

I think it's important that dignity is given to the terminally ill, at all stages. Here, I have found warmth, friendliness and a real caring for the whole family. The team find contentment in the work, supporting one another. The hospice achieves living through dying. Every day means something.

Kay Scott, matron, and Chrissie Gittings confer.

30 Joan Cooper

I am a widow. I live on my own. So I have to do things for myself. This gives you an inbuilt mechanism to go out and seek information. So, I started to ask questions. The first step was to go to the group practice. I went to the desk and asked if they had any information about terminal illness. They said I would need to see the Health Officer. I was taken into a room and sat down with the Health Officer. She asked me for my name and address, and asked me who the patient was. Was it a relative of mine? I told her that I was the patient. She was shocked. She asked if I was alright and would I like a cup of tea? This was one or two hours after I had been given the verdict.

I needed to know what help I could have when I needed it. I have family around me, but they can't do everything. The Health Officer said there were Macmillan nurses, but did I realize that there was a waiting list? I thought, I didn't have to queue up to get into this world, but I'm going to have to queue up to get out of it.

Since then I have read two books a month about my illness. I needed to know what it was to be able to cope with it. I could sit at home and cry with my family, but that would be no good. I am happy to say there is now a social worker attached to the practice. She can act as a go-between. She is coming up to the hospice today to see what it is all about.

*

They call us the Larries – the ones from Laramie. A friend of mine had an accident. He was in an ambulance. A junior doctor wanted to put a plaster over his hole*. He showed him the card†. "If you do that," he said, "you will kill me." He goes round now giving talks to junior doctors and nurses.

---

*Joan carries a card which explains that she has a Laryngectomy, her voice box removed.
†The hole is a stoma. It is to breathe through.

31 Pam Harris

I'm a retired early individual, who has some time to spare for working at the hospice.

One of my jobs is to collect items from members of the public who wish to have their goods sold in the hospice shop on Yorkshire Street. To do that I come up to the hospice, pick up the van and pick up the addresses that are left here at the hospice. And I go down to the shop and pick up the addresses for which collections have been asked from the shop.

It's very interesting, I'm beginning to know Rochdale quite well. I have been as far up as Whitworth, almost into Todmorden, quite often in to Heywood and Middleton, sometimes up to Shaw. So I get around a bit and meet some quite interesting people.

In many senses I do act as a sort of counsellor, I suppose, although I've had no particular training in this field. It's just a question of remembering what happened when your own family were bereaved, and how you reacted to it, and how you think they might react to it.

So quite often I speak with people who've lost their husband, wife, sister, brother, whatever. I can often find that I spend about ten minutes with each person. I could probably spend longer, but the progress of the day is such that I can't. But nevertheless it seems to give something of a helping hand.

I remember one in particular where a sister had died and the one who was left was concerned that she probably hadn't done enough for her sister, because she lived far away. I think this was probably a valid reason for distress on the part of the lady who remained. She was concerned that she hadn't done her best. So I had to argue the toss with her that she probably had done her best. The lady, incidentally, who'd died, had not died in the hospice because, strangely enough, even in Rochdale, the hospice wasn't known. I can't understand that, despite all the publicity we get, people still don't know about the hospice. But I was able, I think, to give a bit of consolation to the lady who was clearing out her sister's house.

In most cases, it's a question of clearing out somebody's house, not always, but quite often. It's an odd sort of feeling that all their treasures are being dumped, if you like, in the shop. All their clothes, perhaps not all their treasures. There's always something that's going to surprise you amongst the goods that come in.

I say counselling in inverted commas, it's just listening, and many people have no time to listen these days. To listen to people who are in trouble, or, who have no other means of expressing themselves. It might be a cold day, standing on the street with the person, or they might ask you to step inside. More often than not, they don't, you're on the street. It seems to be a worthwhile aspect in the work of the shop, and the work of the hospice, of course.

We've thought for many years, well, for the number of years that the shop has been open, that not only do we provide money for the hospice, we also provide a social service. The people that come into the shop sometimes just want to come in and sit down, and there is one chair, and sometimes they want to buy things, sometimes they want to give things, and some of our customers come in every day, spend something every day. So, it is a need. it's not only a need for the hospice, it's a need for these people.

32   Mary Evans

They take time to get to know you, what kind of person you are. Medication, they ask you questions, if you're alright on one medication, if you're not, they'll change it. They try their best to please you. I dare say they get their awkward ones in. But overall, I've no qualms about the place. I can't put the place down because I find it great. Staff are. Right from coming here. They go out of their way to help you, in any way they can.

You do get one or two voluntary helpers, tend to treat you like children. "Ah, there there now," you know. Other than that, the place, I've no problem at all.

I was a nurse. A private nurse, old people's homes. Night nurse. And in Germany. Geriatrics.

There was one old lady, at Chambermount. And every Friday, she knew when it was Friday, I don't know how she knew, but she knew when it was Friday. It must have been payday, when she was younger. The matron of the place had to give her ten pence, on a Friday. And she used to wait for me coming in, on a night-time. And she used to say, "We'll go to the pub tonight, I've got paid tonight. We'll go to the pub." And I used to have to make up every excuse you can think of, because she couldn't go out or anything. But to her, she were going to the pub.

This particular night, I'd gone in, she said she wanted to go, I said, "No, we can't, it's raining tonight Agnes." "Oh, is it raining?"

"Yeah." "Right." An hour went by, and I went doing my rounds. Looked in, no Agnes. Downstairs, no Agnes. And I eventually found her in the larder, with a tin of Guinness. And she left her ten pence on the side.

I am married to a soldier. We got posted to Wolfenbottle. That's near Hanover. For three years. Then we got posted to Verden, which is near Hanover again, for three years. So I went to B.M.H. Hanover.

It's hard. Very hard. Before you go into marriage, before you get married to a soldier, you've got to realize, that he's on exercise, nearly nine months out of twelve months every year. So you've got to get used to being on your own, and bringing children up on your own. And if they can't handle that, that's why marriages break up.

You have babies, you have children. Your husband's not there to see them walk. He's not there to see them talk. Take their first words, or their first steps, and so on. Well a lot of young girls resent this. You know, "I've been at home for a fortnight with the kids, you've been off." But he hasn't been off. He's been on exercise. He's been working. Where a lot don't realize this. And they can't understand why when he gets back, he wants to have a pint with his mates. (Like he just comes back, "Where are you going?" "I'm going for a pint with the lads." "I haven't seen you for a fortnight." They can't understand that they need that unwinding time.

If you can relate yourself to married life, to a soldier, or to any of her majesty's forces, if you can get used to living on your own and bringing children up on your own, you'll find you have a fulfilled life, really. Get to see loads of places. There's nothing stopping you from getting on a train and going to see another place, just because your husband's not there. It makes you very independent. It makes you grow up.

*

At thirty-four years of age, my stomach blew up like a balloon. I looked as though I was pregnant. So I went to the doctor's. They related me to Oldham Infirmary for tests for a fortnight. They did all kinds of tests to try to unblock the fluid, and they didn't succeed. So they sent me down to Crumpsall for a scan. They sent me then back to the infirmary, on the Wednesday morning, and the doctor came to me on the Wednesday afternoon, to tell me they were transferring me to Boundary Park, and operating on me on the Thursday. Didn't say why or anything. I was transferred to Boundary

Park. They operated on me on Thursday. And I was out of it for about six days. I didn't know what had happened or anything.

From Boundary Park I had appointments for Christie's Hospital. We went down to Christie's Hospital. Professor Crowther told me I had cancer. And at the time I felt very angry. Like, why me? Why should it be me? But on the other hand, why shouldn't it be me? I'm nobody special. It took me three months to relate to it, to relate to "I've got cancer." And then I thought to myself, well, you have to carry on with life, doing everything you did before, now. Because up to getting cancer, I was fine, healthy. I lived a normal life, went out frequently at night. So that's what I carried on doing. Went out, doing the same things, going swimming and everything.

As the cancer progressed, and various treatments I tried, chemotherapy, six months, loss of hair, wearing wigs — that's another experience you have to get used to, you have to accept — wearing a wig. A lot of people don't like wearing wigs. It's better than going round bald. And then you try interferon. And that treatment, it's as though you've got flu all the time. But you go through the treatments, various treatments, because in the end, they spare you, they're still doing good, they're still making you live. And to live, you'll try anything.

Mary Evans with her daughter Debbie (left) and her niece Kelly.

Various feelings do get mixed up in time. Sometimes you feel like you could kill youself. Do away with yourself. And then you realize that it's wrong. Why should you? You might have another twelve months. You might have another two years. Why end your life now? If you've got something to look forward to, do it. Book a holiday. And aim for that goal. Book it so you're going on holiday in eight months time. So, you'll live for eight months. Then you go on holiday and come back. And then make another goal that you've got to live for.

More so if you've got children, they make you live. You've got to live for your children. You know your husband can cope, but your children can't. So you live for them. You get there in your mind. It's not what you do, it's how you do it. If you carry on your life, like you did before somebody said that word, cancer, you'll live a lot longer.

Useful Addresses

Springhill Hospice,
Broad Lane,
Rochdale,
OL16 4PZ
Tel:- 0706 49920

British Association of Cancer
United Patients,
121/123 Charterhouse Street,
London EC1M 6AA
071-608-1661
Counselling Service 071-608-1038

Cruse: Bereavement Care,
Cruse House,
126 Sheen Road,
Richmond,
Surrey TW9 1UR
081-940-4818

National Carers Association,
29 Chilworth Mews,
London W2 3RG
071-724-7776

Women's National Cancer
Control Campaign,
128 Curtain Road,
London EC2A 3AR
071-729-1735
Helpline Counselling 071-729-2229

National Association of
Laryngectomee Clubs,
2nd Floor,
11 Elvaston Place,
London SW7 5QG
071-581-3023

Help the Hospices,
34 Brittania Street,
London WC1
071-278-5668

Imperial Cancer Research Fund,
PO Box 123,
Lincoln's Inn Fields,
London WC2A 3PA
071-242-02200

North West Arts,
4th Floor,
12 Harter Street,
Manchester M1 6HY
061-228-3062

Hospice Arts,
Forbes House,
9 Artillery Lane,
London E1 7LP
0732 359171/771699